joy
THE
BAKER
cookbook

joy wilson

joy

THE BAKER

cookbook

100

simple and comforting

recipes

HYPERION

NEW YORK

Library of Congress Cataloging-in-Publication Data

Wilson, Joy.
    Joy the baker : 100 simple and comforting recipes / Joy Wilson. — 1st ed.
        p.   cm.
    ISBN 978-1-4013-1060-8
1. Cake. 2. Desserts. 3. Baking. I. Title. II. Title: 100 simple and comforting recipes.
TX771.W477 2012
    641.8′653 — dc22
            2011015044

Hyperion books are available for special promotions and premiums. For details contact the HarperCollins Special Markets Department in the New York office at 212-207-7528, fax 212-207-7222, or email spsales@harpercollins.com.

BOOK DESIGN BY SHUBHANI SARKAR

First Edition

10 9 8 7 6 5 4 3 2 1

THIS LABEL APPLIES TO TEXT STOCK

We try to produce the most beautiful books possible, and we are also extremely concerned about the impact of our manufacturing process on the forests of the world and the environment as a whole. Accordingly, we've made sure that all of the paper we use has been certified as coming from forests that are managed, to ensure the protection of the people and wildlife dependent upon them.

to dad

Thank you for waking me up at four in the morning to help you roll out pie crust, for stirring maple syrup into my breakfast cereal, and for teaching me the value of a good buttermilk biscuit. Thank you for showing me exactly what love looks like. You're a force in my life.

to michael

Once upon a time, I dreamed of starting a food blog. I didn't have a camera, a computer, or the slightest inkling of how to get such a thing off the ground. You changed all that. Thank you for your unfailing support. We made this!

contents

joy
THE
BAKER
cookbook

introduction

"Hey Dad," the phone call started, "can I have Aunt DeDe's pound cake recipe? I want to put it on my blog."

"What's a blog?" my dad replied.

"It's an Internet thing, Dad. I dunno, I'll tell you later," I said, trying to stay on topic.

"Well, if I give you the recipe, will you bring some of the cake over later?" Dad is a negotiator.

"Sure. But only if I can bring over a few loads of dirty laundry, too." I'm a negotiator also.

"Deal," Dad said.

I spent most of 2008 waking up at 3:30 in the morning. I use the term "in the morning" loosely, as that hour is actually the middle of the night. I'd shuffle into my chef coat, wiggle into my kitchen clogs, and make my way to my job as a baker.

I should tell you now that being a baker is not glamorous. I'd wear my hair in a bun, and invariably find it dusted with flour by the end of the day, my mascara would sometimes singe my eyes shut if I poked my head too far into the oven, and I can't even count the number of scars I have from burning myself on hot pans.

I should also tell you that being a baker in those early-morning hours has been the most joyous and satisfying career. There was always a warm cookie to sneak off the speed rack, a fresh doughnut to "taste test," and a kitchen full of surly baker people to pass the hours with. Cupcakes are boxed up for parties. Fresh scones are paired with black coffee; muffins are bought, shared, and enjoyed. Being a baker was entirely satisfying.

I didn't just fall into a baking career. I've been baking with my father and aunt since I was old enough to stand on a stool in the kitchen. My dad had me helping him roll out pie crusts just as soon as my little fingers could help him hold the rolling mat. My aunt DeDe, who was blinded by a brain tumor, also taught me what was what in the kitchen. From spice cakes to tea cookies, I learned to get the feel for baked goods, moving beyond the actual recipe. My mom, the cake decorator, taught me how to make a perfectly spreadable frosting and how to take cakes from good to great, with pink borders and sugar flowers. Surrounded by all of that love, support, flour, and butter, it's no wonder I became a baker.

I should be honest: I'm not a classically trained pastry chef. I'm a self-taught, family-taught, and taste-bud-taught baker, and truly passion driven. Ultimately, I really like cakes and cookies, so I taught myself how to make them.

Can I tell you a secret? I faked my way into those bakery jobs. It's not that I couldn't do them, it's just that I didn't have the specific culinary school experience most bakeries require. Instead of fluffing my résumé or lying about culinary school, I would simply bring a fresh batch of chocolate chip cookies or a big box of brownies with chocolate buttercream frosting to the interview. It was always better to show off my skill rather than just talk about it. The trick worked, and I found myself on the early-morning baking shift before I knew it.

Joy the Baker, the blog, was born in early 2008. I borrowed a camera and a computer, and had a friend teach me how to use them. In its early stages, Joy the Baker was a less than graceful place for awkward food photography, personal over-sharing, and recipes . . . always recipes. Three months in, I marveled at the thirty-two readers I'd amassed. A year later, I was humbled by the one thousand people that would visit the site daily. Today, I'm in awe of the community that Joy the Baker has brought together. There are people in the world that are just as crazy as I am about butter, sugar, and flour. Thank heavens! It's amazing what food and photography can inspire.

I approach baking in a nonconventional way. When I decide to bake something, I think not about the actual item that I want to bake, but how I'm feeling and what I want to re-create: an occasion, a person, a season. It's the emotion rather than the actual item that inspires something beautiful and delicious. People connect with the mood more than the food.

Almost everyone loves dessert. People are just looking for an excuse to eat cake for breakfast. If you have the power to coax something beautifully sweet out of your kitchen, it's as though you have a magic wand in your hands. With a recipe and a mixing bowl, I promise that you will have the power to delight your daughter with birthday cupcakes, sway your husband with chocolate chip cookies, and surprise your coworkers with homemade coffee cake. There's an undeniable satisfaction in putting a sweet treat in someone's hand and enjoying the resulting ear-to-ear grin.

This cookbook is your magic wand. All of these treats are meant to be shared—unless of course you're feeling greedy, which I also totally understand and sometimes support.

Each recipe in this book is meant to be approachable, comforting, and, of course, delicious. I approach my kitchen with a lighthearted spirit, and I want everything that comes out of it to feel free of pretension or complication. These recipes aim to be fun to make and a joy to eat.

I encourage you to use this book to celebrate life and love. They're both made better with sugar, butter, and cream. There's an undeniable connection between sweet treats and smiles; I hope this cookbook inspires both.

1

joy the baker kitchen tips

from a sometimes messy, sometimes understocked, mostly delicious kitchen

Let me be honest—sometimes my kitchen is a hot mess. I don't have all the latest and greatest kitchen gadgets. Heck, sometimes I don't even have buttermilk! Despite these shortcomings, I'm absolutely determined to make every single sweet treat my crazy brain dreams up.

Baking isn't about high-tech gizmos. It's about stepping into your kitchen with a monster sweet tooth and coaxing something beautiful out of the oven. Grab a bowl and a whisk from amid the hodgepodge of nesting bowls and burnt wooden spoons. It's okay if you don't have a fancy-colored mixer. I promise that with a little determination, butter and sugar can be creamed with just a bowl and a handheld spoon. Fish out your favorite apron, too—there's nothing wrong with looking cute while you bake. Here's a peek inside my kitchen cabinets along with a few helpful tricks that I use to save myself yet another trip to the grocery store.

In-a-Pinch Buttermilk

Let me put a nasty rumor to rest. Buttermilk is not simply milk with chunks of butter in it. Who told you that anyway?

Buttermilk is a slightly sour dairy product. Traditionally, buttermilk was the liquid left over from churning soured cream into butter. Nowadays, commercially manufactured buttermilk is made by adding an acid to low-fat milk. It's the acid that gives buttermilk its sour taste and slightly thickened consistency.

When it comes to baking, buttermilk is a dream come true. The acid in the milk reacts to the baking soda and produces some seriously soft and tender cakes and biscuits.

Thankfully, if you're fresh out of buttermilk, or forget to pick it up at the store because you wrote out a long and detailed list and left it on your kitchen counter, you can simply just make your own soured milk and keep on baking!

NOTE: I have always had the most success with the first two options, as they have a good amount of acid to react with baking soda. The others will surely do in a pinch.

Lemon and Milk

1 cup

In a 1-cup measuring cup, add a scant 1 tablespoon of fresh lemon juice. Top juice with 1 cup skim, low-fat, or whole milk. Stir and let rest for 2 minutes. If you need more than 1 cup buttermilk, add an additional 1 teaspoon lemon juice per additional 1 cup milk.

Vinegar and Milk

1 cup

In a 1-cup measuring cup, add a scant 1 tablespoon white vinegar. Top vinegar with 1 cup skim, low-fat, or whole milk. Stir and let rest for 2 minutes. If you need more than 1 cup buttermilk, add an additional 1 teaspoon vinegar per additional 1 cup milk.

Yogurt or Sour Cream and Milk

1 cup

Mix ¾ cup plain yogurt or sour cream with ¼ cup milk; stir.

Milk and Cream of Tartar

1 cup

Cream of tartar is the acidic ingredient in baking powder. In this preparation, we're adding the acidity of this powder to milk to fake our way into some buttermilk. To ensure that the mixture doesn't get lumpy, mix 1¾ teaspoons cream of tartar with 2 tablespoons milk until smooth. Add enough milk to make 1 cup.

What the Heck Is Cake Flour?

Good question. Cake flour is bleached flour with a lower protein content than all-purpose flour. Cake flour is made from softer wheat than all-purpose flour, and the lowered protein content creates a very light and tender crumb in cakes and cookies.

I seem to remember my mom always having a box of cake flour tucked away in the refrigerator for birthday cakes. Unfortunately, I'm not as prepared a baker as my mother, and I never seem to have cake flour around when I need it.

While we can't change the very structure of the flour itself, we can fake our way into a lighter flour. Here's the fix:

Set a fine mesh sifter over a medium bowl and lay a piece of wax paper on the counter.

Put 1 cup minus 2 tablespoons all-purpose flour into the sifter. Add 2 tablespoons of cornstarch to the flour.

Sift the mixture into the bowl. Dump the contents onto a piece of wax paper. Return the flour back to the sifter, fit over the bowl, and sift again.

Repeat this process, sifting the flour and cornstarch 3 times.

Am I Seriously Out of Brown Sugar?

I daydream about brown sugar. It's soft, sticky, and has a hint of sweet bitterness. Brown sugar adds depth to every recipe it encounters. It's definitely a staple in my kitchen.

Let's start with the facts. Commercially produced brown sugar is a mixture of granulated sugar and molasses. When sugarcane is refined, two products are made: white granulated sugar and molasses. Dark, syrupy, dense, bitter molasses is a product of the sugar-making process. These days, cane sugar is rinsed, cleaned, and stripped of all its molasses. A portion of molasses is then added back to the sugar to evenly create light or dark brown sugar.

Knowing this, it seems pretty reasonable to make our own brown sugar at home, right?

Here's how:

Mix 1 cup granulated cane sugar with 1 tablespoon unsulfured molasses. I found that mixing with a fork works really well. As the sugar and molasses are mixed, they'll become sticky and clumpy. You might wonder if you've done something wrong. Nope! Stick with it. Continue to stir the mixture and eventually the sugar and molasses will marry into a fluffy, light brown sugar.

For dark brown sugar, add another 1 tablespoon molasses.

Use this brown sugar just as you would the store-bought variety, by pressing brown sugar into a measuring cup with the back of a spoon. Store in an airtight container, or in a sealed bag with the air pressed out.

Do I Really Have to Sift This Flour?

I'll be honest; I have neither the time, nor the desire to sift flour for every recipe I bake. Isn't that just something that my grandma does in the kitchen? Sifting flour is important because it ensures that there are no strange lumps or (gasp!) bugs in your flour. When flour sits in the cupboard for months, it inevitably settles in its container. Sifting helps to aerate the flour. That lightness translates into the finished product. Using a metal sifter or a fine mesh strainer, sift flour onto a large sheet of wax paper, then use a spoon to fill your measuring cup with the proper amount. Bonus: the more time you spend with your ingredients the better you understand them.

I love using a medium-sized fine mesh strainer to sift together all of the dry ingredients necessary for a dessert: flour, leavening powders, cocoa perhaps, and salt. Sifting ingredients together ensures they are well aerated, and helps incorporate flavors. It really takes minimal effort.

How Big Are These Eggs?

They may come in the same cardboard crate, but eggs come in all sorts of sizes: small, medium, large, extra large…heck, jumbo, even. The standard U.S. chicken egg is referred to as a "large" egg. Each large egg is between 57 and 64 grams and has roughly 3½ tablespoons of liquid inside the shell. Extra-large eggs have about 4 tablespoons of liquid inside of them.

Before your eyes glaze over, let me tell you why this is important. Baking is all about ratios. The ratio of liquid to flour and leavening is what makes a baked good a cake and not a cookie.

All baking recipes are made using large eggs unless otherwise stated. This ensures that the standard 3½ tablespoons of liquid is introduced into each recipe per egg. If, for example, a recipe calls for 4 eggs and you add 4 extra-large eggs, you're adding 2 extra tablespoons of liquid to the recipe. That can affect the outcome of your dessert, creating a more dense or wet batter than is intended.

Be sure to use large eggs, for consistent and correct baking habits.

How to Get the Most Flavor Out of Fruit Zest

Here's one of those tricks fancy pastry chefs learn in culinary school.

To get the most flavor out of your lemon, orange, or grapefruit zest, all you need is granulated sugar.

Measure out as much granulated sugar as you need for a recipe. Place it on a large cutting board or clean counter. Zest the prescribed amount of citrus for the recipe and add the zest to the sugar. Using the back of a spoon, or your clean fingers, rub the zest into the sugar. The coarse granulated sugar will release the essential oils of the citrus zest. That's where all the flavor is. As you work the zest into the sugar, you'll create an intoxicatingly fragrant sugar. Once mixed with butter, flour, and eggs, the essential oils released by the sugar will perfume and flavor the entire dish.

Just think…you got that tip without shelling out major culinary school tuition.

How to Get the Bundt Out

I've spent two hours making and baking a beautiful Bundt cake, only to invert the pan onto a cake platter and have only half of the cake leave the pan. Man, oh man! There's nothing worse than a bunked Bundt. Here are some tips on how to get your Bundt cake out, free and clear, every time.

Use a thin metal Bundt pan. These pans heat up quickly in the oven and bake evenly. These are factors when it comes to Bundt removal.

Fat and flour are not optional. Using a paper towel or piece of waxed paper, spread butter or vegetable shortening around the entire inside of a Bundt pan. Don't forget the center ring. Every part of the inside of the pan should be well greased. Add about 3 tablespoons all-purpose flour and shake it around the pan to coat. It's hard to get the center ring, but some is better than none. Nowadays many bakers use those newfangled nonstick baking sprays. Those work mighty fine. Go for it! Add batter and bake immediately.

Once the cake is removed from the oven, allow the cake to rest for 30 to 45 minutes. Don't try to remove the cake from the pan when it's piping hot or stone cold. Bundt cakes are easiest to remove when they're cooled but still warm.

Cross your fingers and place a large plate over the top of the Bundt pan. Using pot holders if necessary, grip the plate to the top of the Bundt pan and invert. Set the plate on the counter and slowly remove the pan. Perfection? Good!

Why Do I Have to Use Cold Butter?

How cold is cold? Cold butter is incorporated into a recipe directly out of a 45-degree F refrigerator.

Cold butter is used to create things like crisp and flaky pie crust and mile-high buttermilk biscuits. In other words, use cold butter to create flaky texture and height in baked goods.

Cold butter is quickly introduced into dough by "cutting" it into the flour mixture. This can be done using a food processor, pastry cutter, two butter knives (though this is my least favorite technique because it takes so long), or your hands. The key to incorporating cold butter into a recipe is to do so quickly. Cold butter needs to be kept cold.

Say you're making a flaky pie crust for a sweet potato pie. Directions specify to cut cold butter into the flour mixture, add the cold buttermilk, and let it rest in the fridge. All of these elements involve cold. See where I'm going with this? Once you roll the crust out and shape it in the pie pan, you'll again let the crust rechill in the fridge before baking. When the crust is nice and cold, throw in the pie filling and jam the whole thing into a hot oven.

Magic happens when a cold pie crust hits a hot oven. The water inside the cold butter bits quickly evaporates, creating both lift and flakes within the pie crust. The water inside of the butter slightly leavens and creates texture within the gluten. This texture is something that only cold butter can provide. It's like delicious science, right?

How to Soften Butter in a Hurry

I want cookies, and I want them exactly now. Unfortunately, my butter is sitting in the refrigerator as hard as a rock. Ideally, butter should be removed from the fridge and left to rest on the counter, at room temperature, for about 2 hours. I've found that leaving butter on the counter overnight is best. But, seriously? We can't always plan ahead like that. To soften butter in a hurry, try one of these methods:

Cut butter into small pieces, and spread the pieces out on a clean cutting board at room temperature. Small pieces will come to room temperature faster than a whole stick of butter. If possible, let the pieces of butter rest for about 30 minutes before using.

Place the butter between two large sheets of waxed paper. Take a rolling pin and beat it until slightly flattened. Roll the butter flat with the rolling pin. Working the butter in this way will help speed up the warming process. Remove the top layer of waxed paper, fold the butter in half, re-cover with waxed paper, and roll again.

Softening butter in a microwave is not ideal. The microwave melts the butter more than it softens it.

Butter is softened and ready to work with if it is easily pressed between two fingers, but is not a melty mess.

How to Brown Butter

Browned butter is one of the best things this world has to offer. It adds a beautiful nutty richness to cookies, cakes, muffins, and frostings.

Place butter in a medium-sized, silver-bottomed skillet over medium heat. You'll need to keep an eye on how the butter is browning, so a silver-bottomed skillet is better than dark cast iron.

Allow butter to melt. Once completely melted, the butter may foam and froth as it cooks. The butter will also create a crackling and popping sound. That's the water cooking out of the butter. No real stirring is necessary. Swirling the pan is fine.

Once the crackling subsides, keep an eye on the butter. The fat solids will begin to brown once the water is cooked out. They do so quickly, so don't multitask. The butter will begin to smell rich and nutty as the fat browns. Once the butter solids reach a rich chestnut color, remove the pan from the heat and immediately transfer the butter to a small container. Make sure to scrape all of the brown bits into the container; they're delicious. Removing the butter from the hot pan will stop it from cooking and possibly burning. Once the butter has cooled to room temperature, use as directed.

How to Make Your Own Vanilla Extract

Dang, vanilla beans are expensive! For this reason, I use every part of the vanilla bean, and rarely throw an empty vanilla pod away. All of my used vanilla pods go toward making homemade vanilla extract. Here's how to make your own:

Clean a mason jar by dipping into boiling water and allow to air dry.

Using a sharp knife, cut lengthwise down the center of 6 vanilla beans, leaving the top ½ inch of the beans uncut, but exposing all of the vanilla inside. You can also add any vanilla pods that you've previously scraped clean of vanilla goodness. There's still tons of flavor in the pod itself.

Put vanilla beans and pods in mason jar, and top with 2 cups vodka or bourbon. Vodka will create a cleaner vanilla extract, and bourbon will add lots of rich character.

Press the vanilla beans down into the alcohol so they are completely submerged. Give the jar a good shake. Seal the jar of vanilla beans and alcohol, and place in a cool, dark spot for 2 months.

Be sure to shake the jar before measuring out desired amount. I use the extract straight from the jar without straining the vanilla beans or seeds.

Continue to add vodka, bourbon, and extra vanilla beans to your mason jar to keep your vanilla extract flavorful. The extract lasts for many months. I've had mine for nearly a year.

How to Season a Cast-Iron Skillet

Natural cast iron is not a nonstick pan. It becomes nonstick through a process of oiling and baking called "seasoning." Once a skillet is seasoned, it's a great nonstick kitchen pan. My cast-iron skillet is a big part of my kitchen. I have one specifically dedicated to cakes, tarts, and all things sweet. With cast iron just for baking, I don't have to worry about cakes baked with a hint of garlic or onions. Here's how to season a cast-iron skillet:

Place racks in the upper third and middle of the oven and preheat to 350 degrees F. Place a foil-lined baking sheet on the middle rack. This will catch any drippings as the cast iron bakes.

Open a kitchen window or turn on the hood fan, as there may be some smoke. I've never had an issue, but you never know.

Approach the cast-iron pan. Is it dirty and crusty? Feel free to give it a good scrub with soap and water. This is usually frowned upon, but it must be clean for seasoning.

Once the cast iron is clean, dry it with a towel.

Place the cast-iron pan over medium heat and rub the bottom and sides of the pan with 1 tablespoon vegetable shortening. Use a paper towel and tongs to easily spread the fat across the hot pan.

Place the oiled pan upside down in the heated oven over the foil-lined baking sheet. Bake the cast-iron pan for 1 hour. Turn off the oven and allow the pan to cool to room temperature. Repeat the seasoning process (minus the scrubbing) 3 or 4 times for best results.

Once well seasoned, try to avoid submerging the cast-iron pan in soap and water. It's best cleaned by adding vegetable oil or shortening to a paper towel and scrubbing the warm cast-iron free of excess food bits. Wipe the pan clean when cooled. If oil and a paper towel just don't cut it, you can clean a cooled cast-iron skillet with water and a scrub sponge. Dry the cast-iron over low heat on the stovetop until warm and no water remains. Once cool, re-season with oil in the oven.

2

pancakes pancakes pancakes

and other lesser breakfast items

Dear Future Husband and Future Children,

We don't yet know one another. In my impatience, I've taken to writing you letters. We have a whole, big exciting life to live together, and I want you to have as much information as possible going into this adventure.

First, I need you to know that I love breakfast. I love breakfast as much as I love shoe shopping, baby cats, and the smell of chubby baby thighs. I'll be the first person out of bed in the morning to put on the coffee, whip up some batter, throw on the eggs, and fry the bacon.

All you have to do is bring your sleepy faces to the table to eat breakfast every morning. Easy, right?

As it turns out, the only thing I like more than cooking breakfast, is watching people I love enjoy it. So, do we have a deal, Future Husband? Are you in for this, Future Children?

Great! I'm glad that's all settled.

I give you my love, in the form of breakfast.

Love,
Joy

oatmeal raspberry ginger scones

makes 12 scones

There were some dark days in my baking career when I couldn't bake an appetizing scone to save my life. Amazingly, the days of flat, dry, and downright dangerous hockey puck scones came to an end when I adapted this recipe from Dorie Greenspan.

My trick? Take frozen butter to a box grater. The cold flakes of fat help the dough come together with less handling, producing a pleasingly tall, biscuit-like scone. The dark days are over, friends!

Fresh raspberries are best for this recipe, as they don't break down as quickly as frozen and thawed berries.

NOTE: Try not to overmix the berries into the dough, or the baking powder and raspberries will react and create strangely blue scones.

1 egg

½ cup cold buttermilk

1⅔ cups all-purpose flour

1⅓ cups old-fashioned oats

⅓ cup granulated sugar

1 tablespoon baking powder

½ teaspoon baking soda

½ teaspoon salt

¼ teaspoon freshly grated nutmeg

½ teaspoon ground ginger

10 tablespoons unsalted butter, cold

¾ cup fresh raspberries

1 tablespoon finely chopped fresh ginger

Place a rack in the center of the oven and preheat oven to 400 degrees F. Line a baking sheet with parchment paper. Set aside.

Whisk together egg and buttermilk. Set aside.

In a large bowl, whisk together flour, oats, sugar, baking powder, baking soda, salt, nutmeg, and ground ginger.

Using a box grater, quickly grate cold butter until it is all shredded. Using your fingers, quickly incorporate the butter into the flour mixture, breaking the butter pieces into the flour.

If you don't have a box grater, cut the cold butter into small pieces and quickly rub the butter into the dry ingredients until pebbly.

Pour the buttermilk mixture over the flour mixture and stir with a fork until the dough comes together. The dough will be wet and sticky.

Gently fold the berries and fresh ginger into the dough, being careful to not completely break down the berries. Five to eight turns of a spatula should be enough to incorporate the fruit and ginger.

Turn the dough out onto a floured work surface. Flour your hands and begin to press the dough together into a rough circle, about 1½ inches thick.

Use a ¼ cup ice cream scoop to portion out 12 scone dough balls. If you don't have an ice cream scoop, a 2-inch round biscuit cutter will also work well. Place on the lined baking sheet and bake for 20 minutes or until the tops are golden and firm. Transfer to a cooling rack for 10 minutes before serving. Scones are best eaten the day they are made.

brown butter blueberry muffins

makes 12 muffins

Hold up your pinky: we're about to pinky-swear. I pinky-swear that these will be the best blueberry muffins to ever emerge from your oven. Browned butter adds an alluring and slightly nutty depth to these muffins. They also happen to be positively packed with fresh blueberries, topped with streusel, and, well…sent down directly from heaven. Pinky-swear. I promise.

For the muffins:

7 tablespoons unsalted butter

⅓ cup milk

1 large egg

1 large egg yolk

1 teaspoon pure vanilla extract

1½ cups all-purpose flour

¾ cup granulated sugar

1½ teaspoons baking powder

¾ teaspoon salt

2 cups fresh blueberries (If using frozen blueberries, thaw the berries and drain liquid before using.)

For the topping:

3 tablespoons unsalted butter, cold

½ cup all-purpose flour

3 tablespoons granulated sugar

Place a rack in the upper third of the oven and preheat oven to 375 degrees F. Line a muffin pan with paper or foil liners. Set aside.

To make the muffins: melt butter in a small saucepan over medium heat. Keep an eye on the butter. It will melt, froth, and begin to crackle. That's the water cooking out of the butter. The crackling will subside and butter will begin to brown fairly quickly. Remove from heat when butter solids become a medium brown color and butter smells slightly nutty. Immediately pour hot butter into a small bowl, or it will continue to cook and possibly burn in the hot saucepan.

Whisk milk, egg, yolk, and vanilla until combined. Add brown butter and whisk to combine.

Whisk together flour, sugar, baking powder, and salt in a medium bowl. Add milk mixture all at once to the flour mixture and stir gently to combine. Gently but thoroughly fold in the blueberries. Divide batter among prepared muffin cups.

To make the topping: combine all of the ingredients in a bowl and rub together with clean fingertips until crumbly. Sprinkle topping evenly over the muffin batter in the cups.

Bake 18 to 20 minutes until golden and crisp and a skewer inserted into the center of a muffin comes out clean. Cool muffins in the pan for 15 minutes before removing. Serve warm or at room temperature.

Muffins will last, at room temperature in an airtight container, for up to 3 days. I like them best the day they're made.

vegan pumpkin pecan bread

makes two 8x4-inch loaves

I love when vegan recipes trick me into thinking they are packed full of butter, eggs, and cream. Lord knows I don't seem to be able to go a day without those indulgences. Here, however, pumpkin and spices are the stars of the show. These loaves bake up moist and fragrant and full of autumn flavors. Since this recipe makes two loaves, I love to wrap and freeze a loaf for that unexpected holiday hostess gift or to whip out for last-minute company. It's all-purpose perfection.

3¾ cups all-purpose flour

2 cups packed light brown sugar

2 teaspoons baking soda

1 teaspoon baking powder

1 teaspoon salt

1 teaspoon freshly grated nutmeg

1 teaspoon ground cinnamon

1 teaspoon ground allspice

½ teaspoon ground cloves

1 (15-ounce) can pumpkin puree

1 cup vegetable or canola oil

⅓ cup pure maple syrup

⅓ cup water

1 cup chopped pecans

8 whole pecan halves, for garnish

Place a rack in the center of the oven and preheat oven to 350 degrees F. Grease and flour two 8x4x3-inch loaf pans and set aside.

In a large bowl, whisk together flour, sugar, baking soda, baking powder, salt, and spices. In a medium bowl, carefully whisk together pumpkin puree, oil, maple syrup, and water.

Add the oil mixture all at once to the flour mixture. Use a spatula to fold the ingredients together. Make sure to scrape the bottom of the bowl well, finding any stray bits of flour and sugar that might have been left behind. Fold in the chopped pecans.

Divide the batter between the prepared pans and arrange 4 whole pecan halves on the top of each loaf.

Bake for 1 hour or 1 hour and 15 minutes, or until a skewer inserted into the center of each loaf comes out clean. Remove from the oven. Let rest in the pans for 20 minutes, then invert onto a cooling rack.

Serve bread warm, in thick slices. Loaves can be wrapped and kept at room temperature for up to 5 days. These loaves also freeze well and can be left at room temperature to thaw and enjoy.

single lady pancakes

makes 1 large or 3 small pancakes

I do things any single girl might do. I sleep in the middle of the bed and am selfish with my two favorite pillows. I take long showers because I don't have to save hot water for anyone else. I make a small pot of coffee every morning and I wait until it's just barely warm to drink. It's just me at home. There's no brushing my teeth with someone after watching *Seinfeld* reruns. There's no ordering the steak and fries for two on date night. That's totally okay because I can still whip up a tiny batch of pancakes and enjoy my singularity without a bowl of lonely leftover pancake batter to deal with. Single lady success—hallelujah!

⅓ cup all-purpose flour

2 tablespoons old-fashioned oats

2 teaspoons granulated sugar

½ teaspoon baking powder

¼ teaspoon baking soda

¼ teaspoon salt

5 teaspoons vegetable or canola oil,
    plus additional for the griddle

Dash of pure vanilla extract

¼ cup plus 2 tablespoons buttermilk

Optional (but highly recommended) additions:

1 tablespoon chocolate chips and
    10 banana slices

2 tablespoons toasted pecans and
    3 sliced strawberries

Small handful dried cranberries and
    chopped walnuts

¼ cup fresh blueberries and zest from
    half an orange

Small handful of dried cherries,
    1 tablespoon toasted almond
    slivers, and a dash of almond
    extract

1 tablespoon all-natural peanut butter,
    10 banana slices, and a drizzle of
    honey

In a small bowl, whisk together flour, oats, sugar, baking powder, baking soda, and salt. In a separate small bowl, whisk together oil, vanilla, and buttermilk. Add the wet ingredients all at once to the dry ingredients. Stir to combine. The mixture will be thick. Fold in any of the optional additions you'd like.

Heat a cast-iron skillet or griddle with 1 to 2 teaspoons oil.

If making one large pancake, pour all of the batter into the hot griddle and spread evenly with the back of a spoon. Cook over medium heat until bubbles form and pop on the surface of the batter. Flip. It's okay if it doesn't flip perfectly. It's hard to do . . . and you're the only one enjoying this pancake, right?

If making 3 small pancakes, pour 3 dollops of batter into the hot pan and cook just as you'd do for one large pancake. They're a little easier to flip when smaller.

Cook until golden brown. Place on a plate and top with any extra toppings that make you happy. Maple syrup is nice, too. Pancakes are best served immediately. Enjoy with a good book and a hot cup of coffee.

zucchini and potato pancakes

makes 12 to 16 pancakes

These are the pancakes I make when I'm trying to get away with having pancakes for dinner, but I know I have company coming over. They fry up with just the right amount of veggie, starch, and crunch. I love to serve them with sour cream, a generous sprinkling of sweet paprika, and a small green salad for an early-evening dinner. How's that for classy?

4 tablespoons olive oil

¼ cup finely diced yellow onion

1 garlic clove, minced

2 cups grated zucchini

2 cups peeled and grated potato

1 teaspoon salt

2 large eggs

⅓ cup all-purpose flour

½ teaspoon baking powder

Sour cream or crème fraîche,
  for serving

Paprika and ground cumin, for dusting

Place a medium-sized sauté pan over medium heat. Heat 2 tablespoons of the oil and add onions. Cook onion until it is translucent, then add garlic. Cook for 1 more minute. Place onions and garlic in a small bowl.

Place zucchini and potato along with ½ teaspoon of the salt in a colander over a medium bowl. Let sit for 10 minutes, then press down with a clean towel, squeezing out excess water.

In a medium bowl, whisk eggs. Whisk in the flour, baking powder, and remaining ½ teaspoon salt. Add the cooked onions and garlic, zucchini, and potato, and stir together until well combined.

Place a rack in the upper third of the oven and preheat to 200 degrees F. The oven will keep the pancakes warm as they're being cooked in batches.

In the medium sauté pan used to cook the onions, heat 2 tablespoons olive oil over medium heat. When oil is heated, drop in the batter by rounded tablespoonfuls. Flatten gently with a fork. Cook about 2 minutes, or until golden brown around the edges. Flip and cook for another 2 minutes or until golden. Place on a plate and keep warm in the oven until ready to serve.

Serve with sour cream or crème fraîche and a dusting of paprika and ground cumin. These pancakes are best served immediately, though they can be cooked up and kept in an airtight container in the refrigerator. Reheat in a lightly greased sauté pan the following day.

cornmeal molasses pancakes with blackberry vanilla sauce

makes 16 to 20 pancakes

My dad pours molasses on his pancakes like it's maple syrup. Yiiikes! Just the thought of that makes me cringe. Molasses is intense! I feel like straight molasses on my pancakes would make my brow sweat.

I've incorporated the perfect amount of molasses into these pancakes, just to honor my dad. It gives these pancakes a real depth and richness. I also totally love the warm berry and vanilla topping. Of course, if you're as hardcore as my dad, keep the molasses jar handy—just in case. Wowza!

For the batter:

1 large egg

1¼ cups buttermilk

1 tablespoon unsulfured molasses

1 teaspoon pure vanilla extract

¼ cup (½ stick) unsalted butter, melted and slightly cooled

1 cup all-purpose flour

½ teaspoon salt

½ teaspoon baking soda

2 teaspoons baking powder

½ cup yellow cornmeal

3 tablespoons butter or oil for the griddle

Sprinkling of powdered sugar, for topping

For the sauce:

½ vanilla bean (or 2 teaspoons pure vanilla extract)

1 heaping cup fresh blackberries (if frozen, thaw and drain)

⅓ cup water

2 tablespoons granulated sugar

Pinch of salt

To make the batter: in a small bowl, whisk together egg, buttermilk, molasses, vanilla, and butter. Set aside.

In a medium bowl, whisk together flour, salt, baking soda, and baking powder.

Add the buttermilk mixture to the flour mixture and stir until just combined. Add the cornmeal and stir until just mixed. If the batter is a bit lumpy, that's okay.

Let the batter rest for 10 minutes while you assemble the Blackberry Vanilla Sauce.

To make the sauce: horizontally cut a fresh vanilla bean in half. Split the vanilla bean vertically down the center, revealing tiny vanilla specks. Scrape out the vanilla specks with a small knife and reserve the pod.

In a small saucepan over medium low heat, warm the berries, scraped vanilla bean and pod (or vanilla extract, if using), water, sugar, and salt. Bring to a simmer and cook for 6 to 8 minutes, until enough liquid has cooked off, creating a slightly syrupy sauce. Some berries will be whole; others will have broken a bit. Remove the vanilla bean pod and place sauce in a serving dish to spoon over pancakes.

Place a rack in the upper third of the oven and preheat to 200 degrees F. The oven will keep the pancakes warm as they're being cooked in batches.

To cook the pancakes: heat a cast-iron skillet or griddle with 1 tablespoon of butter or oil. Once hot, drop 2 tablespoons batter onto the greased skillet. When bubbles begin to appear and burst, carefully flip the pancakes. Cook until the bottoms brown.

Place on a plate and keep warm in the oven until ready to serve.

Serve with warm Blackberry Vanilla Sauce and a sprinkling of powdered sugar. These pancakes are best served immediately.

extra crumb coffee cake

makes one 9x13-inch cake

If this coffee cake were a man, I'm convinced it would be the perfect husband. It has the perfect balance of substance and sweet tenderness. The filling brings in just a bit of spice. A little romance (or chocolate) never hurt anyone either, right? The topping is full of extra heart-melting goodness. Just like when hubby picks up dinner on his way home from work, insists on doing the dishes, and lays one of those knee-weakening kisses on you out of the blue. Mmm hmm. Sign me up for the man and the cake, extra topping—please! This recipe is my adaptation of my favorite King Arthur coffee cake recipe.

For the topping:
1¾ cups granulated sugar
½ teaspoon salt
2 cups all-purpose flour
1 tablespoon ground cinnamon
½ cup (1 stick) butter, softened
For the filling:
1 cup packed light brown sugar
1½ tablespoons ground cinnamon

1 teaspoon freshly grated nutmeg
3 teaspoons unsweetened
    cocoa powder
½ teaspoon salt
For the cake:
¾ cup (1½ sticks) unsalted butter,
    softened
1½ cups granulated sugar
⅓ cup packed light brown sugar

2 teaspoons pure vanilla extract
3 large eggs
3¾ cups all-purpose flour
2½ teaspoons baking powder
1¼ teaspoons salt
¾ cup sour cream
1¼ cups whole milk

Place a rack in the upper third of the oven and preheat to 350 degrees F. Grease and flour a 9x13-inch baking pan and set aside.

To make the topping: whisk together sugar, salt, flour, and cinnamon. Add the butter and stir until thoroughly combined and the mixture resembles moist, coarse meal. Set aside.

To make the filling: whisk together the brown sugar, cinnamon, nutmeg, cocoa powder, and salt. Set aside.

To make the cake: in the bowl of a stand mixer with a paddle attachment, beat the butter and sugars together until well combined, about 4 minutes. Beat in vanilla.

Add the eggs, one at a time, beating for 1 minute after each addition. Scrape the bowl down between each egg addition to ensure that everything is properly mixed. In a small bowl, whisk together flour, baking powder, and salt. Set aside.

In another small bowl, whisk together the sour cream and milk. It may be a bit lumpy, and that's okay. On low speed, add ⅓ of the flour mixture to the batter. As it incorporates, add half of the sour cream mixture. Add another ⅓ of the flour mixture and the remainder of the sour cream mixture. Mix until barely incorporated and add the remaining flour. Finish incorporating the dry ingredients with a spatula to ensure that all of the flour is well incorporated.

Spread half of the batter into the prepared pan. Just eyeball it. It'll be just less than 3 cups. Spread batter across the bottom of the pan all the way to the edges. Sprinkle the filling on top of the batter.

Dollop the remaining batter across the top of the filling and use a spatula to spread batter across pan. Use a butter knife to gently swirl the filling into the batter. Just a few strokes is all it takes.

Sprinkle the topping evenly over the batter and bake the cake until it's golden brown, 55 to 60 minutes. Use a skewer to test for doneness; when it comes out clean, cake is done.

Remove from the oven and allow to rest for 20 to 30 minutes before serving. Cake will last, well wrapped, at room temperature for 4 to 5 days.

baked coffee cake french toast

makes one 8-inch skillet or pan

There are few food tortures worse than waiting for an hour outside of my favorite restaurant for brunch on a Sunday morning. It might be the only time in my life that I insist I'm going to perish from sheer waiting. These days, the only brunch anticipation I do is standing in front of my oven, a cup of coffee in hand, waiting for this treat to come out of the oven. This dish can be thrown together the night before and left to rest in the refrigerator. In the morning, top with crumb topping and bake. I swear, coffee cake and French toast were destined to be together, and there's no reason to wait in line for such a pairing. Serve with fresh berries and a touch of pure maple syrup.

For the French toast:

1 tablespoon unsalted butter

10 slices stale white or whole wheat
    sandwich bread

4 large eggs

1 cup whole milk

½ cup buttermilk

⅓ cup granulated sugar

1 tablespoon pure vanilla extract

For the topping:

½ cup all-purpose flour

¼ cup packed light brown sugar

1 teaspoon ground cinnamon

¼ teaspoon salt

¼ cup (½ stick) unsalted butter, cold,
    cut into cubes

Powdered sugar for garnish

To make the French toast: Melt butter in an 8-inch cast-iron (or any oven-friendly) skillet. Coat the entire pan, including the sides of the skillet with melted butter. Remove from heat.

Slice the bread diagonally. Fan and stack the bread atop the melted butter, cut side down, point side up.

In a medium-sized bowl, whisk together eggs, whole milk, buttermilk, sugar, and vanilla. Once well incorporated, pour the custard over the bread slices into the skillet. Gently press the bread slices into the custard to coat; bread slices will not be completely submerged in the egg mixture.

Cover the skillet with plastic wrap and refrigerate for anywhere from 30 minutes to overnight.

Just before you are ready to bake, place a rack in the center of the oven and preheat to 350 degrees F.

To make the topping: whisk together flour, sugar, cinnamon, and salt. Use your fingers to work the butter into the dry ingredients until the butter is in pea-sized lumps. Remove the soaked bread from the refrigerator and sprinkle with crumb topping.

Bake for 20 to 25 minutes, until the custard has set and the bread tops are toasted. Allow to cool for 15 minutes. Sift powdered sugar over the top of the toast and scoop into bowls to serve. Serve with fresh berries if you'd like. This dish is best served the day it is made.

blueberry orange and almond pancakes with orange maple glaze

makes 12 to 16 small pancakes

Every pancake serves its purpose. The Single Lady Pancakes are just for you; it doesn't matter how misshapen or funky they come out. Top them with bananas and chocolate and they're always perfect. Cornmeal Molasses Pancakes are suitable for you and a few friends. They're full of flavor and class, but still relaxed enough to be welcoming on a weekend morning. These Blueberry Orange and Almond Pancakes are for mothers. Your mother, the mother of an important man in your life, your mother's mother…across the board, they all love these pancakes. It must be the orange and blueberry combination. It suggests breakfast at the Four Seasons. Bonus points if you serve these on nice china atop white linens. That's just a "pro" tip.

For the Pancakes:

1 cup all-purpose flour

1 tablespoon granulated sugar

1 teaspoon baking powder

½ teaspoon baking soda

½ teaspoon salt

1 large egg

¾ cup buttermilk

¼ cup fresh orange juice

2 teaspoons orange zest

Scant ¼ teaspoon almond extract

½ to ¾ cup fresh blueberries
 (or frozen, thawed and drained)

3 to 4 tablespoons butter, for griddle

For the glaze:

1½ cups powdered sugar

3 tablespoons fresh orange juice

1 tablespoon pure maple syrup

Place a rack in the upper third of the oven and preheat oven to 200 degrees F. The oven will keep the pancakes warm as you bake them in batches.

To make the pancakes: in a medium bowl, whisk together flour, sugar, baking powder, baking soda, and salt.

In a small bowl, whisk together egg, buttermilk, orange juice, zest, and almond extract.

Whisk the buttermilk mixture into the flour mixture until just combined. Fold in the blueberries. Let batter rest for 5 minutes while the griddle heats.

Over medium heat, melt 1 tablespoon of the butter in a cast-iron skillet or griddle. Spoon 2 tablespoons batter into the hot pan and cook until golden brown on both sides, about 2 minutes per side.

Place pancakes on an ovenproof plate and store in the oven to keep warm while you cook the rest of the batter, adding butter to the pan as needed.

To make the glaze: whisk together powdered sugar, orange juice, and maple syrup. Serve alongside warm pancakes. Pancakes are best served immediately.

carrot cake pancakes

makes 12 to 16 small pancakes

In my quest to turn my favorite desserts into acceptable breakfast dining, I have come up with these Carrot Cake Pancakes. Please don't tell my parents; carrot cake is their favorite cake. I'm afraid they'll ask me to move home and make these for breakfast every day. I don't think I can handle chores and allowance ever again. We had better just keep this between you and me.

For the pancakes:

1 cup all-purpose flour

1 teaspoon baking powder

½ teaspoon baking soda

½ teaspoon salt

½ teaspoon ground cinnamon

½ teaspoon freshly grated nutmeg

Generous pinch of ground ginger

2 tablespoons chopped walnuts
  (optional)

2 tablespoons golden raisins (optional)

1 egg

2 tablespoons packed brown sugar

1 cup buttermilk

1 teaspoon pure vanilla extract

2 cups finely grated carrots

3 tablespoons butter, for griddle

For the cream cheese spread:

4 ounces cream cheese, softened

¼ cup powdered sugar

2 to 3 tablespoons milk

½ teaspoon pure vanilla extract

Dash of ground cinnamon

Place a rack in the upper third of the oven and preheat to 200 degrees F. This will keep the pancakes warm as they're baked in batches.

To make the pancakes: in a large bowl, whisk together flour, baking powder, baking soda, salt, cinnamon, nutmeg, ginger, and, if desired, nuts and raisins.

In a small bowl, whisk together egg, brown sugar, buttermilk, and vanilla. Stir in the carrots.

Pour the buttermilk mixture, all at once, into the flour mixture and stir until just incorporated. Let rest for 5 minutes while you make the cream cheese spread.

To make the cream cheese spread: in a small bowl, whisk the cream cheese until soft and pliable and no lumps remain. Whisk in powdered sugar, milk, vanilla, and cinnamon. If you'd like a thinner consistency, add a dash more milk. Set aside to top the pancakes.

Over medium heat, melt 1 tablespoon of the butter in a cast-iron skillet or griddle pan. Spoon 2 tablespoons batter into the hot pan and cook, flipping once, until pancakes are golden on both sides, about 2 minutes per side.

Place pancakes on an ovenproof plate and store in the oven while you cook the rest of the pancakes, adding more butter to the griddle as needed. Serve warm with cream cheese spread. Pancakes are best served immediately.

bacon black pepper waffles

makes 12 waffle squares

Question: What are you going to sneak bacon into today?

Answer: You're going to sneak bacon inside your waffles (after it is rubbed in fresh cracked black pepper and baked until golden and crisp). The black pepper and bacon add just the right amount of salt and spice to these fluffy and light waffles. It's the perfect balance for sweet maple syrup.

Now the only question remaining is where you're going to take that late-morning nap after this plateful of breakfast.

Answer: On the couch.

For the bacon:

10 slices bacon

2 teaspoons fresh, coarsely cracked black pepper

For the waffles:

3 cups all-purpose flour

1 tablespoon baking powder

1 teaspoon baking soda

1 teaspoon salt

½ teaspoon fresh, coarsely cracked black pepper

¼ cup packed brown sugar

4 large eggs

⅔ cup canola or vegetable oil

2 teaspoons pure vanilla extract

2½ cups buttermilk

NOTE: If you don't eat bacon, subtract the black pepper and add ¼ teaspoon freshly grated nutmeg and ¾ teaspoon ground cinnamon to the batter—the spice is absolutely delicious.

To make the bacon: position a rack in the upper third of the oven and preheat to 375 degrees F. Line a baking sheet with foil and arrange bacon slices in a single layer across the sheet. Sprinkle generously with black pepper. Place in the oven to bake until bacon is brown and crispy, 10 to 15 minutes. Remove from the oven and place bacon slices on a plate lined with paper towels. Once cool enough to handle, chop bacon into bite-sized chunks and set aside while you prepare the waffle batter.

Set your waffle iron on a level, clean surface and turn on to preheat.

To make the waffles: in a large bowl, whisk together flour, baking powder, baking soda, salt, pepper, and brown sugar.

In a medium bowl, whisk together eggs, oil, vanilla, and buttermilk. Add the buttermilk mixture, all at once, to the flour mixture. Stir until just incorporated. Fold in the bacon. Try not to overmix the batter. If a few lumps remain, that's OK.

Cook according to your waffle machine instructions. Serve with warm maple syrup. Waffles are best served immediately.

NOTE: To freeze, allow waffles to cool completely. Store them in pairs in sealed freezer bags and store in the freezer. In the morning, gently reheat waffles in the toaster or toaster oven. Top with butter and maple syrup. Best toaster breakfast ever.

leek and asparagus quiche

makes one 10-inch quiche

Just because I know how to make a perfectly flaky pie crust does not mean it's something I want to do just to get breakfast on the table. The secret to this delicious quiche is its puff pastry crust. With only a bit of rolling and a quick trim, puff pastry transforms into a decadent and ultra-flaky quiche-and-veggie delivery system. Try to get your hands on some all-butter puff pastry as it tastes miles better than the hydrogenated oil pastry crusts.

1 tablespoon olive oil

1 cup leeks, thinly sliced
   from the whites to the
   pale green flesh

2 cups asparagus, sliced into
   ½-inch rounds

1 sheet frozen puff pastry
   (from a 17¼-ounce package),
   thawed but still cold

1¼ cups whole milk

1 cup heavy cream

6 large eggs

1 teaspoon salt

Pinch of ground nutmeg

1 cup grated Gruyère cheese

¾ teaspoon coarsely ground
   black pepper

Position a rack in the upper third of the oven and preheat oven to 350 degrees F.

In a medium sauté pan over medium heat, add oil and leeks. Sauté leeks until just translucent, about 4 minutes. Add the asparagus rounds and cook until bright green, about 3 minutes. The vegetables don't have to be entirely cooked through; they'll cook more in the oven. Remove pan from heat and set aside.

On a lightly floured work surface, unfold the cold puff pastry. If the seams tear and separate, just press back together with your fingers. With a floured rolling pin gently roll the puff pastry, extending the dough about ½ inch on all sides. Fit the pastry into a 10-inch pie pan (see note). Using a small, sharp knife, trim puff pastry so that ¼ inch of dough hangs over the sides. Place in the refrigerator to chill while you assemble the filling.

In a large bowl, whisk together milk, cream, eggs, salt, and nutmeg. Whisk in ½ cup of the cheese.

When ready to bake the quiche, remove the pie plate from the refrigerator and fill with the cooked leeks and asparagus. Pour the egg mixture over the vegetables, and top with the remaining ½ cup cheese and the pepper.

Bake for 45 to 60 minutes. Quiche will puff up in the oven when done. It'll sink down again once it cools. Let quiche rest for 1 hour before serving. Serve warm or cool. Quiche will last, well wrapped in the refrigerator, for up to 3 days.

NOTE: If you only have a 9-inch pan to work with, the puff pastry crust will still work wonders, and you'll just have a bit of filling left over.

toasted coconut dutch baby with banana and pineapple

makes one 10-inch skillet pancake

Let's pretend we're on one of those fancy spa vacations in Hawaii. You know, the kind of vacation where you do yoga all morning then get served fancy juices and a wholesome breakfast on the beach. The kind of vacation where your only concern is which bathing suit to wear to happy hour. What? You've never been on one of those vacations? Me neither. These pancakes might be as close as I ever get.

Dutch Baby Pancakes brown and puff like a popover in the oven. They're absolutely gorgeous for the first 3 minutes out of the oven, and then they begin to deflate. Serve this pancake piping hot and puffed, with warm maple syrup.

¼ cup sweetened shredded coconut	3 large eggs, at room temperature	1 banana, sliced into rounds
⅔ cup whole wheat flour	⅓ cup granulated sugar	1 cup fresh pineapple chunks
⅛ teaspoon ground cinnamon	⅔ cup whole milk	
Pinch of salt	¼ cup (½ stick) unsalted butter	

Place a rack in the upper third of the oven and preheat oven to 400 degrees F. Spread coconut on a baking sheet and bake until lightly toasted, about 4 minutes. Keep an eye on the coconut as it bakes and stir if the edges brown before the center of the pan. Coconut burns quickly. Once browned, remove from the oven and allow to cool. Place the cast-iron skillet in the oven to heat.

In a medium bowl, whisk together flour, cinnamon, salt, and 2 tablespoons of the cooled toasted coconut.

In a medium bowl, whisk together eggs and sugar until thick and pale. Add milk and whisk to combine.

Add the milk mixture, all at once, to the flour mixture and stir to combine. Mixture will be thin.

Carefully remove the hot cast-iron skillet from the oven. Place butter in the pan to melt. Return the pan to the oven to help the butter melt faster. Remove from the oven and tilt the pan to swirl butter all along the bottom and sides of the pan.

Pour pancake batter over the melted butter and immediately return to the oven. Bake for 15 to 18 minutes, or until browned and puffed along the sides and center of the pan.

While the pancake bakes, slice banana and pineapple into bite-sized chunks.

Once the pancake is baked, remove from the oven and immediately top with bananas, pineapple, and remaining 2 tablespoons toasted coconut. Slice into thick wedges and serve immediately, with maple syrup.

giant cinnamon rolls with buttermilk glaze

makes 8 large rolls

Before making these cinnamon rolls, I take a deep breath, and come to terms with the fact that I am going to eat three of these cinnamon rolls warm, straight out of the pan. I take another deep breath and release any guilt that might be associated with such indulgences. Then I take one final deep breath and thank the good Lord for blessing the world with such creations as yeasty dough, cinnamon, sugar, butter, and glaze.

It takes about 5 hours to make these rolls, and 8 minutes to eat 3 of them. It's worth every moment.

For the dough:

1 (¼-ounce) package active dry yeast

½ teaspoon plus ¼ cup
    granulated sugar

½ cup whole milk,
    at room temperature

2 tablespoons packed brown sugar

1 teaspoon pure vanilla extract

1 egg

1 egg yolk

2¾ cups all-purpose flour, plus about
    ¾ cup more for kneading

¾ teaspoon salt

½ cup (1 stick) unsalted butter,
    softened

For the filling:

½ cup granulated sugar

½ cup packed light brown sugar

½ cup finely chopped pecans

¼ cup golden raisins (optional)

1 tablespoon ground cinnamon

½ teaspoon salt

Pinch ground cloves

3 tablespoons pure maple syrup

½ cup (1 stick) unsalted butter, melted

For the icing:

2 cups powdered sugar

¼ cup buttermilk

To make the dough: in the bowl of a stand mixer, combine yeast and ½ teaspoon of the granulated sugar. Heat ¼ cup water to 115 degrees F. The water will feel just warm to the touch. Add to the yeast mixture, stir to combine, and let sit until frothy and foamy, about 10 minutes. If the yeast does not foam and froth, start over with new yeast.

Add remaining ¼ cup granulated sugar, milk, brown sugar, vanilla, egg, and egg yolk. Beat with a wire whisk until well combined. Fit the bowl onto the mixer along with a dough hook. Add the 2¾ cups flour and the salt and mix on medium speed until the dough just begins to come together. Turn the mixer to medium-high and knead the dough for 4 minutes.

Add the softened butter and continue to knead for 6 minutes. The dough will be wet and sticky. Place the dough on a well-floured surface and knead ⅓ to ½ cup flour into the dough. The dough will still be just slightly sticky. That's okay. Set the dough to rest in a large greased bowl. Cover bowl with plastic wrap and drape a kitchen towel over the bowl. Allow the dough to rise in a warm place for 1½ to 2 hours or until doubled in size.

While the dough rises, make the filling.

To make the filling: in a medium bowl, combine sugars, pecans, raisins (if desired), cinnamon, salt, and cloves. Stir in the maple syrup and set aside.

When the dough has doubled in size, dump it out of the bowl onto a heavily floured work surface. Gently knead the dough until it is no longer sticky, adding about 3 tablespoons of flour as needed. Knead the dough for about 2 minutes. Place a clean kitchen towel over the dough and let it rest on the counter for 5 minutes.

Using a floured rolling pin, roll the dough into a 10x20-inch square. Turn the dough so that the short sides are parallel to you. You're going to roll from the short side of the dough.

Brush the dough with ¼ cup of the melted butter. You'll use the rest of the butter after the rolls are baked. Pour all of the filling onto the dough. Spread evenly, leaving a 1-inch border at one of the short edges of the dough so the roll can be properly sealed. Lightly press the filling into the dough.

Roll the dough into a tight cylinder. Pinch all along the edge to seal. Place dough, seam side down, on a cutting board. Cut roll into 8 equal slices.

Arrange the slices, cut side up, in a greased 9x13-inch baking pan. Each roll will have a few inches of space on all sides. Cover with plastic wrap and leave to rest in a warm place for 2 hours. You can also refrigerate the rolls overnight. Just be sure to bring them to room temperature before baking the next morning.

Place a rack in the upper third of the oven and preheat to 375 degrees F. Bake until golden brown and bubbling, about 30 minutes. Drizzle with the remaining ¼ cup melted butter just after the rolls come out of the oven.

To make the icing: while the baked rolls cool slightly, whisk together powdered sugar and buttermilk until smooth. Drizzle over the warm rolls and serve.

whole wheat honey and goat cheese drop biscuits

makes 8 to 10 biscuits

You know those mornings when you can't bear the thought of kneading a single thing or flipping a single pancake? When your cat wakes you up at 4:30 a.m. and you stub your toe trying to fill his food bowl… and you have company coming over for an early brunch…and all you want to do is sleep like a big baby in your bed? I know those mornings. These biscuits are the cure-all solution for those types of mornings.

Whole wheat flour makes these drop biscuits dense and nutty. Honey adds a touch of alluring sweetness and goat cheese is delicious any time. This is easy biscuit goodness. Serve with fruit jam or soft scrambled eggs. These biscuits are totally versatile.

2 cups whole wheat flour

3 teaspoons baking powder

¼ teaspoon baking soda

1½ teaspoons salt

¼ cup (½ stick) unsalted butter, cold, cut into cubes, plus more for the pan

4 tablespoons crumbled goat cheese

1 cup buttermilk, cold

2 tablespoons honey, plus more for topping

Place a rack in the upper third of the oven and preheat to 400 degrees F. Place a 10-inch cast-iron skillet in the oven as it preheats.

In a medium bowl, whisk together flour, baking powder, baking soda, and salt. With your fingers, quickly incorporate the cold butter and goat cheese until the flour resembles coarse meal. Some of the butter and cheese chunks will be the size of small pebbles; others will be the size of oat flakes. Make a well in the center of the flour mixture.

Whisk together buttermilk and honey. Honey may not completely blend into the buttermilk; that's okay. Pour the buttermilk into the well of the flour mixture. Use a fork to blend together the wet and dry ingredients. Mix until all of the flour is incorporated and no dry flour remains. Set aside.

Remove the hot skillet from the oven and add 1 tablespoon butter. Swirl the butter around the bottom and sides of the pan until butter is melted and pan is coated.

Spoon batter by the ¼ cupful into the hot skillet. About 6 biscuits will fit into the 10-inch skillet. Biscuits should have about an inch of room separating them, but will bake up to touch one another. That's great!

Place in the oven to bake for 14 to 16 minutes, until golden and tops appear dry and slightly firm. Remove from the oven. Let rest for 5 minutes. Repeat with the remaining batter. For a glossy finish, brush the biscuits with slightly warm honey. These biscuits are best served immediately, but will last for up to 3 days, well wrapped, at room temperature.

cheddar chive and jalapeño biscuits

makes 10 to 12 biscuits

Biscuits don't care if you decide to sleep in on a Saturday instead of going to an early-morning yoga class. They don't mind if you drank too much wine last night or if you have morning breath. Biscuits won't love you less if you spill coffee on the morning paper and it doesn't faze them if you gobble down five of their biscuit friends at breakfast. Biscuits are silent, perfect, nonjudgmental, buttery breakfast friends.

These are deliciously fluffy buttermilk biscuits. Adding cheese, chives, and jalapeños makes them all the more enticing. They are perfect with a fried egg, delicious with salted butter, and pretty dang good just plain.

The spice from the jalapeño is hiding in the seeds. If you want a spiceless biscuit, just scrape out all the seeds before chopping. Be sure to wash your hands after you handle peppers. You don't want the spice to sneak its way to your eyes or nose.

3 cups all-purpose flour

1 tablespoon granulated sugar

4½ teaspoons baking powder

¾ teaspoon cream of tartar

¾ teaspoon salt

¾ cup cold buttermilk,
    plus more for topping

1 egg

¾ cup cheddar cheese,
    cut into small cubes

1 medium jalapeño, seeds partially
    removed, diced small

3 tablespoons diced chives

¾ cup (1½ sticks) unsalted butter, cold,
    cut into small cubes

Coarse sea salt for topping

Place a rack in the center and upper third of the oven and preheat oven to 425 degrees F. Line 2 baking sheets with parchment paper and set aside.

In a large bowl, whisk together flour, sugar, baking powder, cream of tartar, and salt.

In a small bowl, whisk together buttermilk and egg.

Toss together the cheddar cheese, jalapeño, and chives. Set aside.

Add butter to the flour mixture. With your fingers or a pastry blender, work the butter into the flour, breaking the small cubes into smaller bits. Once the butter is well incorporated into the flour mixture, the flour will resemble coarse meal. Some chunks will be the size of small pebbles, others will be the size of oat flakes.

Toss the cheese mixture into the flour mixture. Create a small well in the center of the flour mixture and add the but-

termilk mixture all at once. Toss together with a fork making sure that all of the flour bits are moistened by the buttermilk. Mixture will be shaggy. Dump the biscuit dough onto a lightly floured counter and knead for 8 to 10 minutes, just to bring it together into a 1½-inch-thick circle.

Cut biscuits into squares or use a 2½-inch circle biscuit cutter to cut rounds. If you don't have a round biscuit cutter, you can use a knife to cut the dough into 12 small squares. Gather dough scraps, knead lightly, and cut out more biscuits until batter is gone. Place biscuits on prepared baking sheets, brush with buttermilk, sprinkle with sea salt and bake for 12 to 15 minutes.

Biscuits are best the day they're made, but can be wrapped, stored at room temperature, and served the next day as well.

coffee bacon

makes 8 to 12 slices

If breakfast were a high-impact game that had big muscle-bound players in gear, and referees with whistles in striped shirts, I'd surely be called out of bounds on this recipe, or get some sort of flag thrown at me. I mashed two of my favorite breakfast items into one breakfast side: coffee on bacon and baked it. The result is a crisp, salty, slightly sweet, subtly coffee-flavored treat. The coffee flavor is not entirely distinct, but adds an exciting depth to the bacon, while the molasses adds a touch of sweetness to complement the salt. I understand if you're skeptical, but game on!

8 to 12 slices uncooked bacon

¼ cup freshly ground coffee

¼ teaspoon chili powder

2 tablespoons packed brown sugar

2 tablespoons molasses

1 tablespoon water

Layer cascading bacon slices atop one another so the fat is on top. Place bacon on top of a piece of plastic wrap or brown butcher paper.

In a small bowl, stir together ground coffee, chili powder, brown sugar, molasses, and water. Spread the mixture on top of the bacon slices, pressing in with the back of a spoon. The coffee topping will only be on the top, fatted rim of the bacon. Wrap the bacon and coffee in the plastic wrap or butcher paper and place in the fridge. Let sit for 2 hours or overnight.

When ready to bake, place a rack in the center of the oven and preheat to 375 degrees F. Line a baking sheet with parchment paper and lay separate bacon slices on the paper in a single layer. If you prefer, you can wipe off some of the ground coffee marinade before baking. The majority of the coffee will only be on the top layer of the bacon slice.

Bake bacon until browned and crisp, 14 to 17 minutes, or until bacon has reached your desired crispness. Remove from oven. Let cool on the pan for 5 minutes, then remove with tongs and serve immediately. I love this recipe with Cornmeal Molasses Pancakes and Warm Blackberry Vanilla Sauce. Divine!

toasted oat smoothie

makes 1 large or 2 small smoothies (about 3 cups)

I liken adding toasted oatmeal to a smoothie to adding volumizing mousse to my thin, mousy hair. Oat-meal gives the smoothie body and shape, flexible hold and shine. Wait…no. Ground toasted oatmeal added to a fruit smoothie adds a subtle nuttiness, a natural thickness, and healthy, belly-filling properties.

Toasting oatmeal brings out its nutty and earthy qualities. Grinding oatmeal in a blender is super simple. There's no reason *not* to sneak it into a morning smoothie. This smoothie is perfect for when you're just not in the mood for buttery biscuits.

¼ cup raw oatmeal (quick-cooking or old-fashioned)

1½ cups soy, almond, or cow's milk

1 frozen banana, cut into 2-inch chunks

½ cup frozen blueberries

2 teaspoons brown sugar, honey, or agave syrup

Place a rack in the center of the oven and preheat to 350 degrees F. Place oatmeal on a baking sheet and bake for 12 to 15 minutes, until oats become fragrant and just slightly browned. Oats won't brown much, but will smell fantastic.

Place oats in a blender, cover, and blend on high until oats become a powder. Some oat bits will be larger than others; that's totally fine.

Remove all of the oats from the blender and measure 2 tablespoons for the smoothie. Reserve the rest of the oats for another smoothie.

Place milk, 2 tablespoons oat powder, banana, blueberries, and brown sugar in the blender. Blend on high until all ingredients are well incorporated. Serve immediately. Feel healthy.

kale spinach banana peanut butter smoothie

makes 1 large or 2 small smoothies (about 3½ cups)

A girl cannot survive on biscuits and bacon alone. I know; I've tried. My thighs got big. Thank goodness I can blend kale into a smoothie. Having one of these green power smoothies for breakfast makes up for all of the sugary things I eat throughout the day. This smoothie does not taste of kale and spinach. It's fruity-sweet and has just a touch of peanut butter protein. If you are skeptical, try this smoothie and surprise yourself. I'm thankful for this smoothie and so are my thighs.

1 heaping cup chopped kale leaves	1½ cups soy, almond, or cow's milk	2 teaspoons honey
1 heaping cup spinach leaves	1 frozen banana, cut into 2-inch chunks	1 tablespoon all-natural peanut butter

Remove kale leaves from their rough center stalk and coarsely chop. Clean spinach leaves thoroughly and remove any thick stalks.

In a blender, mix kale, spinach, and milk until no large kale bits remain, about 45 seconds. Stop blender and add banana, honey, and peanut butter. Blend until the banana is thoroughly combined.

Enjoy immediately and feel super healthy.

oatmeal cookie pancakes

makes about 3 dozen small pancakes

These are the pancakes that I serve to large groups of people that I love. Whether it's a big family brunch, a summer morning with friends, or Christmas breakfast, these cookie-flavored pancakes are comforting and such a joy to watch people inhale.

1½ cups all-purpose flour

¾ cup old-fashioned oats

2 tablespoons packed brown sugar

2 teaspoons baking powder

1 teaspoon baking soda

1 teaspoon salt

¾ teaspoon ground cinnamon

Big pinch freshly ground nutmeg

2 large eggs

2 cups buttermilk

1 tablespoon pure maple syrup

¼ cup (½ stick) butter, melted
and cooled plus more for the
griddle

⅓ cup golden raisins

Place a rack in the center of the oven and preheat to 200 degrees F. This will help keep the cooked pancakes warm while you finish the entire batch.

In a large bowl, whisk together flour, oats, brown sugar, baking powder, baking soda, salt, and spices. Set aside.

In a medium bowl, whisk together eggs, buttermilk, maple syrup, and melted butter. Add the buttermilk mixture, all at once, to the flour mixture and fold together with a spatula until all of the flour is incorporated. Fold in the raisins. Let stand for 5 minutes.

Heat griddle over medium heat and add a touch of butter to melt. Spoon or pour batter onto the hot griddle. Heat until the bottom is browned and the top is bubbly. Flip and cook through, about 2 minutes on each side. Place on a heatproof plate in the oven to rest until ready to serve. Serve with pure maple syrup and a smile. Pancakes are best served immediately.

3

i need a hug, or a brownie. maybe both.

super comfort, straight from the oven to your aching heart

Remember when your mom sat you down for "the talk"? The talk all about how life was perfect, always fair, and nothing bad ever happened? Oh wait... you didn't have that talk? Yeah, me neither.

Life isn't always fair. It is rarely, if ever, perfect. That's just how the cookie crumbles. Luckily we have tools: butter, sugar, flour, and chocolate. I've baked my way through countless heartbreaks, a handful of failed midterms, and two downright embarrassing job interviews.

Chocolate pudding can most definitely mend a broken heart. Flunked tests require an entire pot of rice pudding. When I didn't get that big bakery job that I wanted, I ate kettle corn for 3 days straight. It fixed me right up.

This collection of recipes makes me feel like I'm home under my favorite blanket, or like I just bought a new tube of lipstick. They are as comforting as wearing a great pair of jeans, and as satisfying as a perfect hair day. Comfort comes in all shapes, sizes, and sweetness levels.

Sometimes we need a hug; sometimes we need brownies. Most times, we need both.

chocolate brownie cookies with white chocolate and roasted macadamia nuts

makes 2 dozen cookies

I cannot be left alone with either a package of white chocolate chips or a bag of roasted macadamia nuts. These two things seem to just gravitate toward my mouth by the handful. It's not a low-fat situation, to be sure. These cookies are soft, fudgey, and dense. They're not to be taken lightly. The dark chocolate base is studded with white chocolate and roasted, salted macadamia nuts. To say that these cookies are dangerously delicious is a true understatement.

8 ounces bittersweet chocolate chips
   or coarsely chopped chunks

3 tablespoons unsalted butter

1 cup all-purpose flour

¼ teaspoon baking powder

¼ teaspoon salt

1 cup granulated sugar

1 teaspoon instant espresso or
   coffee powder (optional)

1 teaspoon pure vanilla extract

3 large eggs

¾ cup white chocolate chips or chunks

¾ cup macadamia nuts,
   roasted and salted (see note)

NOTE: If you buy raw macadamia nuts, toss them in 1 teaspoon olive oil and ½ teaspoon salt. Roast at 350 degrees F for 8 minutes, or until the nuts are lightly golden. Allow to cool before folding into the cookie batter.

Place racks in the upper third and middle of the oven and preheat oven to 325 degrees F. Line 2 cookie sheets with parchment paper and set aside.

Gently simmer 2 inches of water in a medium saucepan. Place bittersweet chocolate and butter in a medium-sized, heatproof bowl and place the bowl over, not touching, the simmering water, creating a double boiler. Melt the chocolate and butter together until butter is melted. Remove from the simmering water and stir until chocolate is completely melted. Allow the chocolate to cool.

In a large bowl, whisk together flour, baking powder, and salt. Set aside.

Whisk the granulated sugar, espresso powder, and vanilla extract into the warm chocolate mixture. Whisk in the eggs one at a time until well incorporated. Add the chocolate mixture, all at once, to the flour mixture. Fold to incorporate. When

flour just begins to disappear into the chocolate mixture, add the white chocolate and macadamia nuts. Fold thoroughly. Batter will feel thick.

Dollop batter by the tablespoonful onto prepared baking sheets. Bake for 11 minutes (the cookies are best slightly underdone). Let rest for 5 minutes on the baking sheet before removing to a cooling rack. Cookies will keep in an airtight container, separated in layers by a piece of waxed paper, at room temperature for 5 days.

brown butter
chocolate chip cookies

makes 2½ dozen cookies

My dad started working on the perfect chocolate chip cookie about ten years ago. Two years into his experimentation, there was an unspoken expectation that my father would bring chocolate chip cookies to every family gathering he attended. The man made chocolate chip cookies darn near every weekend. My dad reached perfection about five years into his chocolate chip cookie journey. He really accomplished a lovely cookie.

This is not that recipe. Crazy, I know. See, while my dad was openly perfecting his cookie, I was on the sidelines secretly perfecting my own chocolate chip cookie. I made it. I won't tell you how long it took me to come up with this gem. I don't want to hurt anyone's feelings.

What's so special about these cookies? Butter is incorporated two ways: creamed with sugar, and melted and browned. Browned butter adds an alluring nutty caramel flavor to the cookies. The traditional flavor of the old-fashioned chocolate cookie is preserved—it's just made a little bit better.

1 cup (2 sticks) plus 1 tablespoon unsalted butter, softened	½ cup packed light brown sugar	1 teaspoon baking soda
1 cup granulated sugar	1 large egg	½ cup coarsely chopped walnuts or pecans
1½ teaspoons pure vanilla extract	1 large egg yolk	1 cup (6 ounces) bittersweet
1 teaspoon molasses	2¼ cups all-purpose flour	chocolate chips
	1 teaspoon salt	

Brown 1 stick plus 1 tablespoon butter according to directions on page 11. Once butter is browned, place in a bowl to cool slightly.

In the bowl of a stand mixer fitted with a paddle attachment, cream the remaining 1 stick of butter with the granulated sugar. Cream on medium speed until light and fluffy, 3 to 5 minutes.

Add the vanilla extract and molasses, and beat until incorporated. Once the brown butter has cooled slightly, pour into the creamed butter mixture, along with the brown sugar. Cream for about 2 minutes until well incorporated. Add the egg and egg yolk, and beat for 1 more minute.

In a medium bowl, whisk together flour, salt, and baking soda.

Add the flour mixture, all at once, to the butter mixture and beat on low speed until the flour is just incorporated. Remove the bowl from the stand mixer, and fold in the walnuts and chocolate chips with a spatula or wooden spoon.

Cover the bowl with plastic wrap and allow to chill in the refrigerator for 30 minutes while the oven preheats.

Place racks in the upper third and middle of the oven and preheat to 375 degrees F. Line 2 baking sheets with parchment paper. Roll tablespoons of dough into balls and space about 2 inches apart on the baking sheet. A small ice cream scoop works well.

Bake cookies for 12 to 14 minutes until lightly browned on the outside, but still soft and tender in the center. Feel free to rotate the sheets halfway through baking, switching the sheets on the racks.

Remove from the oven and allow to rest for 5 minutes on the baking sheet before removing to a cooling rack or immediately sharing with your friends. Cookies will keep, in an airtight container, for up to 5 days.

mini pumpkin
black and white cookies

makes about 32 cookies

These Black and White Cookies are such little treasures. It seems that every Black and White Cookie I've ever had has been about the size of my head. I'm all for giant cookies, but good grief!

These pumpkin cookies are soft, cakey, and scented with cinnamon. I topped them with dark chocolate ganache and cinnamon glaze. Wrap these frosted cookies individually, and you'll be a hero to many.

For the cookies:
2 cups all-purpose flour
1½ teaspoons baking powder
1 teaspoon baking soda
½ teaspoon salt
1 teaspoon ground cinnamon
2 large eggs
1 cup granulated sugar

½ cup vegetable oil
1 (15-ounce) can pumpkin puree
1 teaspoon pure vanilla extract
For the cinnamon glaze:
2 cups powdered sugar
½ teaspoon ground cinnamon
1 tablespoon light corn syrup
1 teaspoon pure vanilla extract

Up to 1 teaspoon water
For the chocolate glaze:
4 ounces semisweet chocolate chunks
   or chips
3 tablespoons unsalted butter
Pinch of salt
1 tablespoon light corn syrup

Position a rack in the center of the oven and preheat to 325 degrees F. Line 2 baking sheets with parchment paper and set aside.

To make the cookies: in a medium bowl, sift together flour, baking powder, baking soda, salt, and cinnamon. Set aside.

In a large bowl, whisk together eggs and sugar until well incorporated and slightly pale, about 2 minutes. Add the oil, pumpkin, and vanilla, and carefully whisk until completely incorporated.

Add the flour mixture to the pumpkin mixture and fold together with a spatula until no dry flour bits remain.

Dollop tablespoonfuls of batter onto the baking sheet, keeping about 2 inches between each cookie. Spread the cookie batter slightly with the back of a spoon or a butter knife, creating a 2-inch cookie circle.

Bake cookies for 12 to 14 minutes until just cooked through. Use a skewer to test the center of the cookie if necessary. When the skewer comes out clean, the cookies are done.

Allow cookies to rest on the pan for 10 minutes before using a thin spatula to remove cookies to a cooling rack to cool completely before frosting. While cookies are cooling, make the glazes.

To make the cinnamon glaze: whisk together all ingredients until smooth. Add up to 1 teaspoon water to thin glaze. Set aside.

To make the chocolate glaze: place a small heatproof bowl over, but not touching, a small saucepan of simmering water. In the bowl, melt chocolate and butter. Stir until melted then remove the bowl from the heat. Stir in the salt and corn syrup and set aside.

Cookies should be completely cooled before frosted. Take a baked cookie, flip it over, and wipe any excess crumbs off the bottom. The bottom of the cookie will become the top of the cookie. With a butter knife, spread cinnamon glaze on half of the cookie. With a separate butter knife, frost the other side of the cookie with chocolate glaze. Set the cookie on its top to harden slightly before wrapping. I like to wrap each cookie individually in small squares of plastic wrap.

Cookies will keep at room temperature for up to 4 days.

cinnamon sugar rice pudding

makes 4 to 6 servings

I've been dumped, failed tests, and gotten written up at work. I've had fender benders, dropped my phone in the toilet, and locked my keys inside my car. I mean, really, haven't we all!?

None of that matters, because this rice pudding heals all wounds. This recipe is perfectly starchy and creamy, and the cinnamon sugar brings all the comfort that you could ever want.

Rice pudding can be served warm or cold. I will always and forever consider it to be the most comforting food on Earth. If you happen to have any left over, please consider it an appropriate breakfast food.

For the pudding:

2 cups water

1 teaspoon orange zest

¼ teaspoon salt

1 cup long-grain jasmine rice

3 cups whole milk

½ cup granulated sugar

1 teaspoon ground cinnamon

2 tablespoons unsalted butter

For the topping:

1 teaspoon cinnamon

3 tablespoons granulated sugar

To make the pudding: in a large saucepan over medium heat, bring the water to a boil. Stir in orange zest, salt, and rice, and stir. Return to a boil, cover the saucepan, and turn heat to simmer. Cook the rice until all the water is absorbed, about 15 minutes.

Remove the cooked rice from the saucepan and place in a bowl. Using the same saucepan over low heat, warm the milk, sugar, and cinnamon. If cinnamon clumps a bit just use a whisk to beat the clumps out. They should work themselves out by the time the pudding is complete.

When the milk is warm and the sugar has dissolved, add the cooked rice back to the pot. Stir often as the milk cooks down and the rice becomes creamy. This should take about 20 minutes. Just as the rice pudding finishes cooking, stir in the butter. Allow pudding to rest and cool before serving. I like serving this pudding cold from the fridge the following day. Stir in up to 1 cup more whole milk to loosen the pudding's consistency the next day.

To make the topping: mix together topping ingredients. Scoop into small serving dishes to serve, and sprinkle generously with cinnamon sugar mixture.

grapefruit soufflé pudding

makes one 9-inch pan, or six 1-cup ramekins

Why, hello! So glad you could join us for supper. Oh no, don't worry about being late. There's always unexpected traffic. You two look just lovely tonight, come in! Oh, this dress and pearls I'm wearing? It's just something I threw on at the last minute. The diamond on my finger? Why, thank you for noticing. Yes, it's just something Henry surprised me with. It's so large, I hardly ever wear it. Come in, come in! I'm just about to slice the lamb and I can't wait until you try dessert. Divine!

This dessert is for company. It's classic, and fancy enough to make me feel like I'm the kind of lady who owns pearls and diamonds and throws dinner parties with roasted lamb. Despite its fancy attitude, this soufflé is also comforting enough to serve to your husband in sweats.

This pudding treats egg yolks and egg whites differently. Separating the eggs and reincorporating them back together creates a two-tiered dessert. The bottom layer is a fragrant and bright citrus pudding while the top layer is a light and fluffy grapefruit soufflé. The combination is classy and downright exciting.

¾ cup plus 2 tablespoons
    granulated sugar
2 tablespoons grapefruit zest

3 tablespoons unsalted butter,
    room temperature
3 large eggs, separated
⅓ cup all-purpose flour

¼ teaspoon salt
⅓ cup fresh grapefruit juice
1 cup whole milk
⅛ teaspoon cream of tartar

Place a rack in the center of the oven and preheat to 325 degrees F. Bring a teapot of water to a boil. You'll use this to make a water bath—hot water that surrounds the pudding while it bakes. Butter six 1-cup ramekins or a 9-inch baking dish and set aside. Find a larger pan that can hold all the ramekins or the baking dish.

Place the ¾ cup of the sugar in a medium bowl with the grapefruit zest. With the back of a spoon, grind the zest into the sugar. This will release the essential oils from the zest and create a fragrant and flavorful sugar.

Place the fragrant sugar in the bowl of a stand mixer fit with a paddle attachment and beat with the butter for 1 minute. Add the egg yolks one at a time, beating on medium speed until fluffy and slightly lighter in color, about 2 minutes.

Add the flour and salt, and beat until combined. Alternately add the grapefruit juice and the milk and mix at medium speed until well incorporated. Mixture will be loose and soupy. Place mixture in a large bowl and set aside.

Clean the mixing bowl very well and dry completely. Add the egg whites and beat on medium-high speed until frothy. Add the cream of tartar and beat until soft peaks form. Gradually add the remaining 2 tablespoons sugar and beat until stiff peaks form.

Gently fold the stiff egg whites into the grapefruit mixture in three additions. You don't want the egg whites to be completely broken down, so fold gently, retaining some of the fluff.

Carefully pour the batter into the prepared ramekins or baking dish. The batter does not rise much during baking, so you can fill it pretty high.

Place the ramekins or baking dish in the larger baking pan. Open oven door, place baking pan (with pudding cups or dish inside) into the oven, but sticking out just enough to still work with it. Pour the tea kettle of warm water into the larger baking dish, filling until the hot water reaches about halfway up the ramekins or baking dish. Carefully push the baking dish into the oven. Bake ramekins for 25 to 30 minutes, or larger pan for 35 to 40 minutes until the top of the soufflé is just barely browned and a wooden skewer inserted into the top layer comes out clean.

Pudding can be served warm or at room temperature. This pudding is best the day it is made.

perfect kettle corn

makes about 6 cups

Sure, I make mistakes. Once I was late for a job interview and was turned away. Mistake; lesson learned. Once I didn't study for a statistics test, failed, and had to retake the class. Mistake; lesson learned. Once I was downright rude to a friend and felt like an utter heel until I had the decency to apologize. Mistake; lesson learned.

The common thread through all of these stumbles and mistakes was one thing: kettle corn. After each mistake, I shoveled handfuls of this sweet and salty popcorn into my face. It's part of my process. I know I've learned a lesson when I can't possibly eat another bite. It usually takes a few batches, but I get there.

2 tablespoons vegetable oil	½ cup yellow corn kernels	1 teaspoon kosher salt, or to taste
2 tablespoons unsalted butter	3 tablespoons granulated sugar	

Make sure the pan that you're using is easy to lift and has a tight-fitting lid. You'll need to shake the pan around a bit during popping. Heat oil in a large saucepan over medium heat. Add the butter to melt. Add the corn kernels and sprinkle the sugar as evenly as possible over the unpopped corn. Place the lid on the pot and increase the heat to medium high.

When the corn begins to pop, place 2 pot holders over the lid and the pot handles, securing the lid to the pot. Carefully but deliberately remove the pot from the heat and shake a bit. This will help ensure that the sugar does not burn on the bottom of the pan. Return the pan to the heat as it continues to pop. Shake again every 30 or so seconds to prevent burning.

When popping slows, turn off the heat and take the lid off slightly to release some of the steam. When popping stops completely, remove lid and sprinkle popcorn with ½ teaspoon of the salt. Dump kettle corn into a large bowl and sprinkle with the remaining ½ teaspoon salt. The sugar will still be very hot, so toss with a wooden spoon to prevent any burned fingers.

Enjoy immediately. Be warned: this stuff is totally addictive.

s'mores brownies

makes one 9x13-inch pan

These brownies were inspired by Delilah Bakery in Los Angeles. It turns out that you can turn fudgey chocolate brownies into fond campfire memories with graham crackers and marshmallows. Incredible! When baked, the marshmallows spread out into little pillows of toasted, memory-filled goodness. Who needs boring old walnut brownies? Not us!

1½ cups all-purpose flour

2 teaspoons baking powder

1 teaspoon salt

1 teaspoon instant espresso powder
  or coffee powder (optional)

1 cup (2 sticks) unsalted butter

6 ounces unsweetened chocolate,
  chopped

1¼ cups packed brown sugar

1 cup granulated sugar

5 large eggs

2 teaspoons vanilla extract

1 cup roughly crushed graham crackers

12 large marshmallows

Place a rack in the upper third of the oven and preheat to 350 degrees F. Butter and flour a 9x13-inch baking pan to keep the brownies from sticking to the pan. (Cooking spray also works wonders.) Set aside.

In a large bowl, whisk together flour, baking powder, salt, and, if desired, espresso powder. Set aside.

Place a medium saucepan with 2 inches of simmering water over medium-high heat. In a medium heatproof bowl combine the butter and chocolate. Place the bowl over, but not touching, the simmering water. Stir until melted and smooth.

Remove melted chocolate mixture from the simmering pot and allow to cool for several minutes. Once slightly cool, whisk in sugars. Whisk in eggs, one at a time, until well combined. Whisk in the vanilla then fold in the graham crackers.

Pour batter into prepared pan and dot with the marshmallows. Bake for 30 to 40 minutes or until a skewer inserted into the center comes out with just a few moist crumbs attached.

Marshmallows will be browned and puffy, but will deflate as the brownies cool. Cool for at least 20 minutes before slicing with a sharp knife. Clean the knife under hot running water when the marshmallows begin to stick to the knife. Wrap individually in plastic wrap for storing. Brownies will keep for up to 4 days, well wrapped, at room temperature.

dad's perfect sweet potato pie with no-roll pie crust

makes one 10-inch pie

I have a relationship with this pie. I feel like this pie might be a sibling. My dad has made this pie several times a year for as long as I can remember. Its creation is a downright ritual that my father draws out over several hours, days even. The reality is that this pie is very simple to make once you've boiled the sweet potatoes. It's perfectly spiced with coriander, and is a beautiful substitution for pumpkin pie. I don't fight with this pie like I occasionally fight with my sister, but I might love it just as much.

2 medium sweet potatoes
    (or 2 cups mashed)
¾ cup packed brown sugar
1¼ teaspoons ground coriander
½ teaspoon freshly grated nutmeg

½ teaspoon ground cinnamon
¼ teaspoon salt
¼ cup (½ stick) unsalted butter, melted
2 (5-ounce) cans evaporated milk
    (about 1¼ cups)

3 large eggs
½ cup granulated sugar
1 tablespoon pure vanilla extract
1 Easy No-Roll Pie Crust (p. 72)

In a large saucepan over medium heat, boil sweet potatoes in their skins until potatoes are very soft and tender. Test with a thin, sharp knife. If there is any resistance, boil the potatoes longer. Remove potatoes from the water and allow to cool on a plate or wire rack.

When cool enough to handle, peel potatoes, cut into chunks, and place in a large bowl. Mash potatoes thoroughly with a potato masher. There should be no lumps.

Measure 2 cups of potato and place in a medium-sized pot over low heat. Add the brown sugar, all of the spices, salt, butter, and 1 can, or half, of the evaporated milk. Cook for 5 minutes, whipping with a wire whisk until butter and brown sugar are melted down, and the mixture is well blended and starts to bubble. Remove from heat and let mixture cool in the pot.

In a large bowl, beat the eggs with a fork. Add the remaining can of evaporated milk, granulated sugar, and vanilla and beat until creamy. Add the cooled sweet potato mixture to the egg mixture, and whisk well. Mixture can be refrigerated overnight or used immediately. I love to refrigerate the mixture because I think it helps develop and mellow the flavors.

Place a rack in the center of the oven, place a cookie sheet on the rack and preheat oven to 400 degrees F.

Pour filling into unbaked, 10-inch pie crust and place pie on cookie sheet in the oven. Bake for 10 minutes at 400 degrees, then lower oven to 325 degrees and bake for 50 to 60 minutes, or until the pie crust is browned and the center of the pie is no longer loose or jiggly.

Remove from the oven and allow to cool to room temperature before slicing and serving.

Sweet potato pie lasts, well wrapped, in the refrigerator for up to 4 days.

easy no-roll pie crust

makes one 10-inch pie crust

Pie crust can be a little intimidating. Between cutting the butter into the flour and the cold water, a tiny bit of kneading and just the right amount of rolling, there are a lot of steps that can get wonky. I've found a way to make things a bit easier: take away the rolling! This pie crust comes together with your fingers and a mixing bowl, then gets pressed into the pie plate. You'll feel as if you have a secret weapon up your sleeve.

Keep in mind that because this is a press-and-bake pie crust, it is only used as a bottom crust.

2¼ cups all-purpose flour

1 teaspoon salt

3 tablespoons granulated sugar

¼ teaspoon baking powder

6 tablespoons unsalted butter, frozen

1 heaping tablespoon cream cheese, cold

3 tablespoons milk, cold

¼ cup plus 2 tablespoons canola or vegetable oil

In a medium bowl, whisk together flour, salt, sugar, and baking powder.

Grate frozen butter on a cheese grater. If you don't have a cheese grater, cut the butter into very small chunks when it is just out of the fridge, then let the butter pieces rest in a bowl in the freezer for 10 minutes to super chill.

Add the frozen butter pieces and cream cheese to the flour mixture and use your fingers to quickly incorporate into the flour. The butter bits will range in size from small pebbles to oat flakes. The mixture will look shaggy.

Whisk together the milk and oil. Add, all at once, to the flour and butter mixture, and use a fork to combine the wet and dry ingredients. Make sure all of the flour is introduced into the liquid. The mixture does not need to come together to form a ball. Leave the dough a bit shaggy and dump into the bottom of a 10-inch pie plate.

With your fingers, press the dough evenly into the bottom of the pie plate and up the sides. Try to create an even thickness along the entire pie plate, but don't worry about your finger indentations. You can't fight that, and the crust will bake up smooth.

Place the prepared crust in the freezer while you prepare the pie filling.

If you're going to prebake your crust, heat the oven to 350 degrees F. Spray a piece of foil with nonstick cooking spray and place greased side down onto the pie dough. Weigh down the foil with uncooked beans and bake for 10 minutes. Remove the foil and the beans and bake for 4 to 6 minutes uncovered, until the crust is slightly golden brown. Remove from the oven and let cool completely before filling.

If you need an unbaked pie crust, simply remove the crust from the freezer, load it up with your filling, and bake according to the recipe.

peanut butter bacon cookies

makes about 2 dozen cookies

I have some tricks up my sleeve when it comes to baking for men: they love bacon. Men are also pretty fond of peanut butter. This may stem from the fact that bachelors eat a lot of peanut butter and jelly sandwiches. Combine bacon and peanut butter and I'm telling you, men will fall all over themselves. It's just a fact.

These cookies are a delicious combination of sweet and salty. The bacon is crisp and the cookies have a crumble crunch. I think they're downright perfect.

8 slices bacon

1 cup all-natural peanut butter

1½ cups granulated sugar

2 teaspoons molasses

1 large egg

1 teaspoon baking soda

Generous pinch of freshly grated
   nutmeg

½ cup coarsely chopped roasted,
   salted peanuts

Place a rack in the upper third of the oven and preheat to 350 degrees F. Line a baking sheet with foil and place bacon slices in a single layer. Bake bacon until cooked through and crisp, 12 to 15 minutes. Remove from the oven (keep the oven on), let cool slightly, then transfer to paper towels to cool completely. When cool enough to handle, coarsely chop the bacon and set aside.

Line a clean cookie sheet with parchment paper and set aside.

In the bowl of a stand mixer fitted with a paddle attachment, cream together the peanut butter, 1 cup of the sugar, and the molasses until thoroughly combined, about 3 minutes. Add the egg, baking soda, and nutmeg, and mix on medium speed for another 2 minutes.

Remove the paddle attachment and the bowl and use a wooden spoon to fold in the bacon and peanuts. Roll the dough into large walnut-sized balls and roll in the remaining ½ cup granulated sugar. Place on lined cookie sheet, and use a fork to make that distinctive peanut butter cookie crisscross pattern. If the cookie dough begins to stick to the fork, dip it in sugar before pressing into cookie. Dough will be a little crumbly, just press together with your fingers as necessary.

Bake for 10 minutes, until lightly browned. Cool on the baking sheet for 5 minutes before transferring to a wire rack to cool completely. Cookies will be crumbly and delicious! Cookies will last up to 5 days in an airtight container in the refrigerator.

banana coconut cream pie

makes one 9-inch pie

I adore banana cream pie, but I'd die for coconut cream pie. Obviously, I thought it was a stroke of genius to put the two together. It's the sort of pie that makes me want to paint my nails, put on some lip gloss, pour myself a cup of coffee, and totally pig out on the pie while feeling girlie and pretty.

For the crust:
¼ cup toasted shredded coconut
1½ cups vanilla wafers
    or graham crackers
¼ cup granulated sugar
⅓ cup butter melted, slightly cooled
For the filling:
1½ cups heavy cream

1½ cups whole milk
½ cup granulated sugar
⅓ cup cornstarch
¼ teaspoon salt
3 large egg yolks
1 teaspoon pure vanilla extract
2 tablespoons unsalted butter
1¼ cups toasted shredded coconut

2 ripe bananas, sliced
For the topping:
1½ cups heavy cream
¼ cup powdered sugar
½ cup toasted shredded coconut
1 ripe banana, sliced

Place rack in the center of the oven and preheat to 350 degrees F. To toast the coconut: spread 3 cups coconut on a cookie sheet and bake for 5 minutes. Remove from the oven and toss coconut with a spoon to ensure that the edges of the coconut don't burn. Cook coconut for another 3 minutes, then remove from the oven to toss. Repeat until coconut is evenly toasted. Remove from the oven and let cool. Keep oven on.

To make the crust: crush vanilla wafers in a zip-top bag with a rolling pin. In a medium bowl, mix together the crushed cookies, sugar, and toasted coconut. Pour the melted butter over the dry mixture and toss with a fork, making sure to evenly moisten all of the dry ingredients. Pour mixture into a 9-inch pie plate and use your fingers to press the crust into the plate and up the sides. Bake for 12 minutes, or until slightly browned. Remove from the oven and let cool completely before filling.

To make the filling: in a medium saucepan, whisk together cream and milk over medium heat and bring to a simmer.

In a medium bowl, whisk together the sugar, cornstarch, salt, and egg yolks. In a steady stream, add a cup of the warmed milk mixture into the egg yolk mixture, whisking constantly. This will help warm the egg mixture and ready it for stovetop cooking.

Pour the warmed egg and milk mixture back into the saucepan and cook over medium heat, whisking constantly. The mixture will thicken and boil. You may also want to use a spatula to scrape the edges of the pan as the mixture thickens so none gets stuck and burned. Whisk until bubbly and very thick, 4 to 6 minutes. Remove from the heat. Add vanilla and butter, and whisk until butter is melted.

Pour thickened milk mixture into a large mesh strainer fit over a bowl. Use a spatula to pass the mixture through the

strainer, removing any nasty lumps. Place a piece of plastic wrap directly on top of the custard and place in the fridge to cool completely, about 2 hours.

Once the custard is cool, remove from the fridge and fold in toasted coconut and banana slices. Pour the custard into the cooled pie crust and prepare the topping.

To make the topping: use the bowl of an electric stand mixer fit with a whisk attachment. Whip cream and powdered sugar to stiff but slightly soft peaks. Dollop whipped cream on top of the pie, using a butter knife to make it pretty. Top with the coconut. Refrigerate until ready to serve. Top with fresh banana slices just before the pie is served. (Bananas get brown and icky if exposed to air too long.) This pie is best eaten within 2 days, and it's amazing with black coffee.

chocolate cookies and cream pudding

makes 5 pudding cups

Is it just me or are you always looking for an excuse to buy a box of Oreo cookies, too? Here is a great reason. In this recipe, creamy chocolate pudding is layered with Oreo cookie-fortified whipped cream. This makes me feel like I'm a kid who can eat all the cookies she wants. Hallelujah and amen!

For the chocolate pudding:

2 tablespoons granulated sugar

2 tablespoons cornstarch

2 tablespoons unsweetened cocoa powder

2 teaspoons instant coffee powder

Pinch of salt

1½ cups whole milk

¾ cup heavy cream

4 ounces milk chocolate, coarsely chopped

1 teaspoon pure vanilla extract

For the whipped cookies and cream:

2 cups heavy cream

¼ cup powdered sugar

1 teaspoon pure vanilla extract

12 chocolate sandwich cookies, crumbled

To make the pudding: in a medium saucepan, whisk together sugar, cornstarch, cocoa powder, coffee, and salt.

Gradually whisk in milk and cream and bring to a low boil over medium-high heat. Whisk constantly. Boil, whisking for about 2 minutes. The cornstarch will thicken at the boiling point. Remove from heat, and whisk in chocolate pieces and vanilla extract. Stir until melted and smooth.

Transfer pudding to a medium bowl, cover with plastic wrap, and refrigerate until set and cool, about 2 hours.

Meanwhile, to make the whipped cookies and cream: in the bowl of a stand mixer fitted with a whisk attachment, beat cream on medium-high speed. As the whipped cream thickens, add the powdered sugar and vanilla.

When the whipped cream creates soft peaks, remove the bowl from the mixer and fold in the cookies.

I like to serve this dessert layered brown and white in a large clear glass vessel, but it's also very pretty in sundae-type glasses for individual servings. Top with cookie crumbles.

"man bait" apple crisp

makes one 9x13-inch pan (or halve for one 8-inch pan)

There are things that I do to attract a mate: shower frequently, run a comb through my hair, wear mascara, grace my face with lip gloss, and wear nice heels. My secret weapon, however, is this apple crisp. It is simply baked apples with cinnamon, oats, and streusel. The secret is in the proportions: lots of apples, with loads of streusel topping. It's the crisp topping combined with the soft baked apples and the flash of a flirty smile that makes this streusel absolutely irresistible. Trust me—this recipe alone is how I'm going to find a husband...when I'm ready for all that.

For the filling:

10 to 12 medium-sized apples (I use a mix of Fuji and Granny Smith)

6 tablespoons granulated sugar

3 teaspoons ground cinnamon

For the topping:

2⅔ cups all-purpose flour

2⅔ cups packed brown sugar

1 teaspoon ground cinnamon

1⅓ cups chopped pecans

⅔ cup quick-cooking oats

1 cup (2 sticks) unsalted butter, softened

Place a rack in the center of the oven and preheat to 350 degrees F. Grease a 9x13-inch pan with nonstick cooking spray or butter.

To make the filling: peel and core the apples and cut into ¼-inch-thick slices. In a small bowl, mix together granulated sugar and cinnamon. Place all of the apple slices in the baking dish, and sprinkle with the cinnamon sugar mixture. Using your hands, toss the apples with the cinnamon sugar until evenly coated. Set aside while you prepare the topping.

To make the topping: in a medium bowl, whisk together flour, brown sugar, cinnamon, nuts, and oats. Work the softened butter into the dry ingredients with your fingertips until the mixture resembles coarse meal. Remove 1 heaping cup of the topping, and sprinkle it over the apple mixture. Toss with your hands to incorporate. Place apple mixture in the prepared pan and spread the rest of the topping evenly over the apples.

Bake the crisp until topping is toasted and apples are bubbling, 55 to 60 minutes. Remove from the oven and let cool slightly. Scoop warm crisp into bowls and top with vanilla ice cream. You'll thank me. I'm sure of it.

hot fudge sauce

makes about 2 cups

When chocolate turns from powder or bar to warm and glossy, I just melt on the inside. I will offer you a warning: making your own hot fudge is terribly easy and awfully addictive. When you run out of ice cream, you'll have the urge to eat this warm chocolate sauce on top of everything in sight, which may include bananas, apples, saltine crackers, and your fingers.

⅓ cup unsweetened cocoa powder

⅓ cup packed brown sugar

½ cup light corn syrup

¾ cup heavy cream (not low-fat milk)

¼ teaspoon salt

½ teaspoon instant coffee
   or espresso powder (optional)

7 ounces bittersweet chocolate,
   chopped

2 tablespoons unsalted butter

2 teaspoons pure vanilla extract

Place a medium, heavy-bottomed saucepan over medium heat. Add cocoa powder, brown sugar, corn syrup, cream, salt, instant coffee (if desired), and half of the chopped chocolate pieces to the pot. Cook, stirring, until the chocolate has melted and everything is smooth, about 5 minutes. Remove the pan from the heat and add remaining chocolate pieces, butter, and vanilla. Stir until smooth and shiny.

   Sauce can be cooled slightly and used warm on top of vanilla ice cream. Store in an airtight glass container for up to 1 week. Reheat in the microwave for a few seconds until your desired consistency is reached.

peanut butter ice cream sauce

makes about ½ cup sauce; enough for 4 sundaes

We now have the technology to make peanut butter pour onto ice cream topped with sliced bananas, chocolate sauce, and whipped cream. What a beautiful world it is. Someone call NASA—this feels pretty epic.

2 tablespoons unsalted butter, melted
½ cup creamy peanut butter
   (natural is best)

¼ cup powdered sugar
Pinch of salt
½ teaspoon pure vanilla extract

1 tablespoon milk or cream

Combine all ingredients in a small saucepan over low heat. Once heated through, peanut butter mixture will be smooth and easily pourable.

   Pour over scoops of vanilla ice cream. Feel free to add chocolate sauce, whipped cream, and a fresh cherry. You're totally worth it.

honey and toasted walnut ice cream

makes about 1 quart

The taste of honey is wonderfully comforting. It reminds me of hot cups of tea, Winnie the Pooh, and pajamas with booty feet. Honey and walnuts make this ice cream ultra-classy, but comforting enough to eat directly from the container with an oversized spoon while watching bad reality TV. Rest easy, I have tested this theory.

1 cup chopped walnuts	⅓ cup honey	Pinch of salt
½ teaspoon vegetable oil	½ vanilla bean, split and seeds scraped	¼ cup granulated sugar
¼ teaspoon salt	(or 2 teaspoons vanilla extract)	1 cup heavy cream
2 cups whole milk	5 large egg yolks	

Place a rack in the center of the oven and preheat to 375 degrees F. On a sheet pan, toss walnuts with vegetable oil and salt. Bake for 7 to 10 minutes, until fragrant and toasted. Remove from the oven, place in a bowl and let cool while you assemble the ice cream custard.

In a medium, heavy-bottomed saucepan over medium heat, mix the milk, honey, and vanilla bean (do not add the extract yet). Heat until just boiling, remove from heat, and cover. Let mixture steep for 10 minutes. Once steeped, remove the vanilla bean.

In a separate medium-sized bowl, whisk together egg yolks, salt, and sugar. Beat with a whisk until thick and pale in color. By hand, this may take about 5 minutes. It's a bit of an arm workout.

After yolks and sugar have been well mixed, slowly drizzle about half of the warm milk into the egg mixture, whisking constantly. You're tempering the eggs, getting them ready to be cooked. Transfer the mixture back to the saucepan and place over medium heat.

Stir the mixture almost constantly with a spatula, being sure to scrape the bottom edges of the pan so none of the custard burns. You'll know the custard is done when the mixture is thick enough to coat the back of the spatula (about 8 minutes).

Remove custard from heat and stir in cream and vanilla extract (if using). Pass custard through a fine mesh strainer and into a clean bowl. Cover with plastic wrap (directly on top of the custard) and cool in the refrigerator for about 2 hours, until cold. Freeze in the bowl of an ice cream maker, according to the manufacturer's instructions. Fold in toasted walnuts at the very end of the churning process.

Ice cream will last for up to 1 week, but is best eaten within days.

almost burnt salted caramel sauce

makes about 1 cup sauce

The French knew exactly what kind of trouble they were getting into when they invented butter, stove-top cooking, sugar, and cream. They had to have known that inventing and perfecting such a combination would surely alter the course of the universe…or at least the course of *my* universe. Wait…the French did invent butter and cooking and sugar and cream, right?

This classic salty caramel sauce is made with good French butter. The quality of butter makes all the difference. Splurge on the good stuff. Cook until aaaaallllmost burnt. The long cooking time creates an alluring depth and slight bitterness to the sauce. It's pretty incredible. I want it on everything, always. This recipe was inspired by my favorite pastry chef, Zoe Nathan of Huckleberry Bakery.

1 cup granulated sugar

2 tablespoons water

1 tablespoon corn syrup

6 tablespoons (¾ stick) good-quality salted butter (I like an Irish or French butter)

½ cup heavy cream, at room temperature

1 teaspoon pure vanilla extract

Place a large, heavy-bottomed pot over medium-high heat.

Add the sugar, water, and corn syrup to the warming pan. Whisk the sugar occasionally as it begins to heat, to ensure that the sugar cooks evenly.

Cook the sugar to a nice dark copper color. The sugar will go from golden to dark copper fairly quickly. To help control the sugar, turn off the heat and move the pot to a cool burner just before you reach the dark color you'd like. The bottom of the pan will still be hot enough to continue to cook the sugar.

Over low heat, whisk butter, all at once, into the copper-colored sugar. When butter is melted, pour in the cream. The mixture will bubble and froth, but keep mixing. When bubbling subsides, add vanilla extract. Stir. The caramel might feel too loose. Don't worry; it will thicken as it cools.

Store in a glass jar in the refrigerator for up to 2 weeks. To thin, warm in the microwave for a few seconds until you reach the desired consistency.

peanut butter and jam milkshake

makes one 2¾-cup milkshake

Why eat a sandwich when you can drink a milkshake? That's what I always say. Actually, I don't say that at all…but this delicious swirled milkshake might have me changing my tune.

Here, we're making two milkshakes: a peanut butter milkshake and a fruity jam milkshake. Swirling them together in a tall glass makes two shakes the complete package. All you need is a big, fat straw to enjoy.

For the peanut butter milkshake:

¾ cup vanilla ice cream

2 tablespoons all-natural
    peanut butter

Splash of pure vanilla extract

½ cup whole milk

For the jam milkshake:

¾ cup vanilla ice cream

2 tablespoons raspberry jam

10 frozen raspberries

½ cup whole milk

To make the peanut butter milkshake: in a blender, combine ice cream, peanut butter, vanilla, and milk. Blend on high until smooth, thick, and creamy. Pour the milkshake into a liquid measuring cup, scrape the blender clean, and place the measuring cup in the freezer.

To make the jam milkshake: in the same blender (you don't even have to rinse it out), combine ice cream, jam, raspberries, and milk. Blend on high until smooth, thick, and creamy. Remove the peanut butter milkshake from the freezer, and alternately pour the peanut butter and jam milkshakes into a large glass. Garnish with a straw and enjoy immediately.

parmesan seaweed popcorn

makes about 6 cups

Popcorn is dinner. Especially if there's freshly grated Parmesan cheese and funky spices on it. On a related note, this is why I try to come over for dinner once a week, Mom…I can only eat so much popcorn.

¼ cup olive oil

½ cup yellow popcorn kernels

¼ cup freshly grated Parmesan cheese

3 tablespoons seaweed sesame rice seasoning (from Whole Foods markets or Amazon.com)

Sea salt to taste

Heat oil in a medium heavy-bottomed saucepan. When oil is hot, add corn kernels. Place a lid over the sizzling popcorn, but place the lid askew, leaving room for the steam to escape. Pop the corn until popping slows to virtually nothing, and then turn off the heat.

Pour half of the popcorn into a large bowl. Top with 2 tablespoons of the cheese, 1½ teaspoons of the rice seasoning, and a sprinkle of sea salt. Top with the remaining popcorn, 2 tablespoons cheese, 1½ teaspoons seasoning, and a dash of salt.

Do not toss, or all of the topping will sink to the bottom of the bowl. Eat all of it, and consider it dinner. Enjoy!

baked chili cheese fries

makes 2 servings

No chapter about comfort food would be complete without a recipe for French fries. Sure, I've baked my way out of heartbreak and disappointment with cookies and puddings, but when it comes down to life's serious bummers, French fries are the only way to go.

These mouthwatering French fries have all the flavor of chili fries without the chili. Grill seasoning, smoky chili powder, and spicy chili flakes make these baked potato slices absolutely irresistible. These are totally my new favorite thing!

2 tablespoons cornstarch	Pinch of cayenne pepper	1 tablespoon grill seasoning
1 tablespoon chili powder	Salt to taste	(I used McCormick)
½ teaspoon paprika	2 medium russet potatoes	½ to ¾ cup shredded sharp
¼ teaspoon ground cumin	2 tablespoons olive oil	cheddar cheese
¼ teaspoon red chili flakes	1 teaspoon Worcestershire sauce	2 tablespoons chopped fresh chives

NOTE: McCormick grill seasoning has salt in it. I didn't need more than a few pinches of additional salt for the potatoes to be super delicious. If you use a grill seasoning without salt, add more salt to your own taste.

Place a rack in the center of the oven, and preheat to 425 degrees F. Line baking sheet with parchment paper, and spray paper with nonstick cooking spray.

In a small bowl, whisk together cornstarch, chili powder, paprika, cumin, chili flakes, cayenne pepper, and salt. Set aside.

Rinse potatoes and peel with a vegetable peeler. You can leave some skin bits on the potatoes if you want to go for a more rustic feel. Using a sharp knife, slice a ¼-inch piece off the potato lengthwise. This will give you a stable base to slice on. Rest the potato, cut side down, and slice potato into ¼- to ⅜-inch planks.

Stack the planks in piles, 2 to 3 planks high, and slice lengthwise into ¼- to ⅜-inch strips. Look at that! French fries!

In a medium bowl, toss the potato strips with olive oil, Worcestershire sauce, and grill seasoning. Sprinkle the cornstarch mixture over the potato slices and use tongs to toss together, making sure that every potato is coated with a bit of cornstarch and seasoning.

Spread potatoes onto prepared baking sheet in a single layer. Bake for 30 to 40 minutes, removing from the oven 2 or 3 times to toss potatoes as they cook. Cook until potatoes reach desired crispiness. Remove from the oven, top with cheese, and return to the oven for just a few minutes to melt the cheese. Remove, and place onto a platter, sprinkle with chives, and serve immediately.

avocado fries

makes 4 small servings

These fried avocado wedges remind me of California sun, beaches, and summertime. While being in a two-piece bathing suit isn't my most favorite memory, fresh and creamy avocados make me think of afternoon margaritas at the beach, which is totally my favorite summertime reminiscence. Fry those avocados, and I'm in heaven. These fries are an enticing combination of rich and creamy, spicy and crispy. They're totally worth the effort to take out the fry thermometer and the quart of oil. These are a treat! This recipe was inspired by *Sunset* magazine.

1 quart vegetable oil

2 medium ripe Haas avocados

2 large eggs

⅓ cup all-purpose flour

¼ teaspoon salt

Pinch of cayenne pepper

1¼ cups panko bread crumbs

Salt, lemon, and cayenne pepper
for sprinkling

Clip a fry thermometer onto a medium heavy-bottomed saucepan and heat oil to 375 degrees F.

While the oil heats, halve, peel, and slice the avocados into long spears; it's okay if the size varies slightly.

In a small bowl, beat together eggs.

In a separate small bowl, whisk together flour, salt, and cayenne pepper.

In a medium bowl, measure out panko crumbs. Set out a clean plate for coated slices.

Preheat oven to 200 degrees F and prepare a pan with paper towels. Keep an eye on your oil. If it's reached 375 degrees, turn to low.

Using one hand and keeping the other hand clean, dip avocado slices in egg, lightly coat in flour mixture, and then coat in bread crumbs. The fries don't need a heavy coating—lightly coated is ideal. Place on a plate until all avocado slices are dipped and ready for frying.

Using tongs, lower 6 to 8 avocado slices into the hot oil. Fry until golden brown. Remove from oil and place on lined baking sheet. Sprinkle with a bit of salt, and place the pan in the oven to stay warm.

Bring the oil back up to 375 degrees before frying the next batch. Continue frying until all avocado slices are golden brown. Remove from the oven, sprinkle with a dash of cayenne pepper and fresh lemon juice. Serve immediately.

4

oh, happy day!

recipes to celebrate, from sheet cake to malted milkshakes

I don't know about you, but in my family, we fight over who gets to make Dad's birthday cake. We bicker about who will prepare the Mother's Day dessert. We arm-wrestle over the right to concoct my sister's graduation cake.

We take our cakes pretty seriously because the lucky baker will, no doubt, be showered with compliments, rose petals, hundred-dollar bills, and a waterfall of diamonds. Actually, the lucky baker will receive none of those things except compliments…which come in a close second to diamonds and dollars.

I suspect that these gorgeous celebration desserts will have you showered in compliments as well: compliments that are just about as sweet as the dessert that inspires them.

texas sheet cake

makes one 15x10-inch cake

This is THE cake to end all birthday cakes in my family. I've enjoyed this cake as a large-toothed little girl, begrudgingly enjoyed it as an intolerable teenager, and chowed it down on college breaks. I plan on enjoying this cake as a crotchety old lady. It's the cake that tastes perfectly familiar, yet thrillingly satisfying every time I eat it.

Texas Sheet Cake is a thin layer of fudgey chocolate cake topped with a warm chocolate and pecan frosting. The cake and the frosting meld together to create a sticky, sweet, classic chocolate cake. It tastes perfectly delicious every single time. My dad once tried to get creative and added mint extract to the cake. Outrage! There was almost a coup. Don't feel the need to make this cake anything more than what it is… because it is perfect.

For the cake:

1 cup (2 sticks) unsalted butter

5 tablespoons unsweetened cocoa powder

1 cup hot coffee (or water)

2 cups all-purpose flour

2 cups granulated sugar

1 teaspoon baking soda

½ teaspoon salt

2 large eggs

1 teaspoon pure vanilla extract

½ cup sour cream

For the frosting:

½ cup (1 stick) unsalted butter

4 tablespoons unsweetened cocoa powder

6 tablespoons evaporated milk

4 to 5 cups powdered sugar, sifted

1 teaspoon pure vanilla extract

1 cup coarsely chopped pecans

Preheat oven to 350 degrees F. Grease a 15x10x1-inch jelly roll pan with butter and flour or nonstick cooking spray. Set aside.

To make the cake: place a medium saucepan over medium heat, whisk together the butter, cocoa powder, and coffee. Cook until butter is melted. Remove from the heat and let rest while you prepare the dry ingredients.

In a large bowl, whisk together flour, sugar, baking soda, and salt. Add the cocoa mixture to the flour mixture, and fold until almost entirely incorporated.

Whisk in the eggs, vanilla, and sour cream until thoroughly combined. Pour mixture into prepared pan and bake for 20 minutes. While the cake is baking, prepare the frosting.

To make the frosting: place a medium saucepan over medium heat. Melt together the butter, cocoa powder, and evaporated milk. When butter has melted, remove the pan from the heat and whisk in powdered sugar. When completely blended, add vanilla extract and chopped pecans.

When the cake is fully baked, remove it from the oven and immediately top the warm cake with the warm frosting. Spread evenly. Let cake set for at least 1 hour before serving. Cake will last, well wrapped, for 4 days at room temperature.

mini chamomile cakes with honey frosting

makes 12 mini cakes or cupcakes

What's not included in the directions to this recipe is this stellar "pro" tip. Wash your face with fancy-smelling soap and put on a fancy-smelling face mask. Prepare cupcakes according to these boring old directions. Bake cupcakes. Put on lip gloss. Feel utterly pretty.

These tender little lady cakes were inspired by the *Hummingbird Bakery Cookbook* and are delicate and beautifully scented. Serve to lady friends with tea.

For the cakes:
¼ cup (½ stick) butter
1 cup all-purpose flour
¾ cup granulated sugar
1 teaspoon baking powder
½ teaspoon baking soda

Pinch of salt
3 tablespoons dried chamomile
   (from tea bags)
½ cup milk
1 large egg
1 teaspoon pure vanilla extract

For the frosting:
2 cups powdered sugar, sifted
1 tablespoon honey
6 tablespoons heavy cream
Pinch of salt

Place a rack in the upper third of the oven, and preheat to 325 degrees F. Line a cupcake pan with paper or foil liners and set aside. You can also grease and flour the cupcake pans and not use any liners.

To make the cakes: in the bowl of a stand mixer fitted with a paddle attachment, cream together butter, flour, sugar, baking powder, baking soda, salt, and chamomile leaves. The mixture will be slightly coarse and sandy when mixed for several minutes.

Whisk together milk, egg, and vanilla.

Pour half of the milk mixture into the flour mixture with the mixer on medium-low speed. Beat until just incorporated. Pour in the remaining milk mixture, and turn mixer up to medium. Beat for 1 minute, until well blended.

Divide the batter between the prepared cupcake cups. There isn't a lot of batter, so you'll only fill the liners up about halfway. You'll also need a spatula to scrape the bowl for remaining batter. This recipe doesn't waste a drop of cake batter.

Bake cupcakes for 17 to 20 minutes or until a skewer inserted in the center comes out clean. Remove from the oven, and allow cakes to cool in the pan for 10 minutes. Remove cakes to cool completely on a wire rack before frosting.

To make the frosting: whisk together sifted powdered sugar, honey, cream, and salt in a medium bowl. Whisk until smooth. Use a butter knife to generously spread the frosting atop the cooled cupcakes. Sprinkle with just a bit of chamomile leaves and arrange on a pretty plate. Cakes will last, well wrapped, at room temperature for up to 3 days.

pumpkin bundt cake with cinnamon glaze

makes one Bundt cake

Pumpkin puree is a wonderful, not-so-secret ingredient. Pumpkin not only adds a gorgeous golden color and enticing flavor, but this friendly squash makes for a foolproof, always moist cake. You can't go wrong with this dessert, especially in the autumn months.

For the cake:

2 cups granulated sugar

2 cups all-purpose flour

2 teaspoons baking powder

2 teaspoons baking soda

¼ teaspoon salt

2 teaspoons ground cinnamon

½ teaspoon ground cloves

½ teaspoon freshly grated nutmeg

½ teaspoon ground ginger

1 cup vegetable oil

¼ cup buttermilk

1 teaspoon pure vanilla extract

2 cups (15-ounce can) pumpkin puree

4 large eggs

1 cup coarsely chopped walnuts,
    plus more for topping

For the frosting:

2½ cups powdered sugar, sifted

1 teaspoon ground cinnamon

6 tablespoons heavy cream

Place a rack in the center of the oven and preheat to 350 degrees F. Grease and flour a Bundt pan, or spray well with nonstick cooking spray. Set aside.

To make the cake: in a large bowl, whisk together sugar, flour, baking powder, baking soda, salt, and spices. Set aside.

In a separate large bowl, whisk together oil, buttermilk, vanilla, and pumpkin puree. When well blended, add eggs one at a time. Beat well in between each addition.

Pour the pumpkin mixture, all at once, into the flour mixture. Use a spatula to fold the mixture together. Scrape the bottom of the bowl well, making sure not to miss any flour bits. Fold in walnuts.

Pour the batter into the prepared pan and bake for about 1 hour, or until a cake tester inserted into the center comes out clean. Remove from the oven and let rest in the pan for about 30 minutes.

Carefully invert the cake onto a cake stand or serving platter, and let cool completely.

To make the frosting: whisk together the powdered sugar, cinnamon, and cream. Drizzle over cooled pumpkin cake and top with walnuts.

peanut butter birthday cake

makes one 2-layer 8- or 9-inch cake

I believe in peanut butter. Is there a way that we could incorporate positive sentiments about peanut butter into the national anthem? Maybe a peanut butter jar on our state flag? No? Hmm…maybe I'll just have to get a puppy and name him Peanut Butter.

This cake is an homage to my love of peanut butter. Its unadulterated peanut flavor is truly over the top. The peanut butter cake is dense, but still moist. It is not a cake to take lightly. The Peanut Butter Cream Cheese Frosting is insanely good. The cream cheese adds a slight tang; a lovely twist to a take-charge cake.

2¼ cups all-purpose flour	¾ cup smooth peanut butter	½ cup packed brown sugar
2 teaspoons baking powder	6 tablespoons (¾ stick)	3 large eggs
1 teaspoon baking soda	unsalted butter, softened	1 cup plus 2 tablespoons buttermilk
½ teaspoon salt	½ cup granulated sugar	

Place a rack in the center and upper third of the oven and preheat to 350 degrees F. Grease and flour two 8– or 9-inch round cake pans. Nonstick baking spray works well, too. Set aside.

In a medium bowl, whisk together flour, baking powder, baking soda, and salt. Set aside.

In the bowl of an electric stand mixer fitted with a paddle attachment, cream together peanut butter, butter, and sugars until fluffy, for 3 to 5 minutes.

Add eggs, one at a time, beating at medium speed for 1 minute between each addition. Stop the mixer and scrape down the bowl as necessary.

With the mixer on low speed, add half of the flour mixture to the butter mixture. Slowly pour in all of the buttermilk. When mixture just starts to come together, add the remaining flour mixture, beating on low speed until mixture just begins to come together. Remove the bowl from the mixer and finish incorporating the ingredients with a spatula.

Divide the batter between the 2 prepared baking pans. Place on 2 racks in the oven. Bake for 15 minutes, rotate the cake pans to alternating racks, and continue to bake for 15 to 25 minutes or until a cake tester inserted in the cake comes out clean.

Let cakes cool in the pans for 10 minutes, before inverting onto wire racks to cool completely before frosting.

Frost cakes with Peanut Butter Cream Cheese Frosting (p. 140), Cream Cheese Frosting (p. 136), or The Best Chocolate Buttercream Frosting (p. 133).

Cake will last, wrapped, in the refrigerator for up to 4 days.

kitchen sink carrot cake

makes one Bundt cake or one 2-layer 9-inch cake

My parents had carrot cake as their wedding cake. Just imagine tiers and tiers of spiced carrot cake surrounded by luscious cream cheese frosting! Divine. These days, it's a cake that I feel so blessed to share with my family.

This cake is warm and moist. It's full of just about everything in the kitchen: fresh carrots, pineapple, coconut, brown sugar, and spices. All of the flavors shine through beautifully in this cake.

3⅓ cups all-purpose flour

2 teaspoons baking powder

1 teaspoon baking soda

1 teaspoon salt

2 teaspoons ground cinnamon

3 large eggs plus 1 egg yolk

1 cup granulated sugar

1 cup plus 2 tablespoons packed
  brown sugar

1¾ cups vegetable oil

1 cup crushed pineapple, drained

2 teaspoons pure vanilla extract

2¼ cups grated carrots

½ cup sweetened shredded coconut

¼ cup raisins or dried cranberries
  (optional)

¼ cup chopped walnuts (optional)

Place a rack in the center of the oven and preheat to 350 degrees F. Grease and flour a 10- or 12-cup Bundt pan or two 9-inch round pans and set aside.

In a large bowl, whisk together flour, baking powder, baking soda, salt, and cinnamon. Set aside.

In a medium bowl, whisk together eggs, yolk, and sugars. Blend with a whisk until well incorporated and slightly thickened. Add the oil and carefully incorporate. This part could get a little splashy. Add the crushed pineapple and vanilla, and stir until incorporated.

Add the pineapple mixture, all at once, to the flour mixture. Fold together with a spatula. When almost incorporated, fold in the carrots, coconut, and (if desired) raisins or cranberries and nuts. Fold until evenly blended. Pour cake batter into prepared pan(s) and bake for 35 to 45 minutes, or until a skewer inserted into the center comes out clean. Let cake cool in pan for 15 minutes before inverting on a wire rack to cool completely before frosting with Cream Cheese Frosting (p. 136). Bake cake layers for 28 to 35 minutes or until a skewer inserted in the center comes out clean. Bake Bundt for 45 to 55 minutes or until a skewer inserted in the center comes out clean.

red velvet marble cake

makes one 2-layer 8- or 9-inch cake

Red Velvet Cake is so 2008. To spice this cake trend up, I've created a marble. Chocolate cake batter is swirled with red velvet cake batter. Yep…I'm trying to create a new food trend: the swirl and marble trend. Let's see how fast it catches on. Frost this cake with either Cream Cheese Frosting (p. 136) or The Best Chocolate Buttercream Frosting (p. 133). Either way, this cake is sure to be the prettiest thing at the party.

For the chocolate cake:

1 cup all-purpose flour

¾ teaspoon baking soda

¼ teaspoon salt

½ cup prepared coffee

⅓ cup plus 1 tablespoon unsweetened cocoa powder

½ cup (1 stick) unsalted butter, at room temperature

½ cup plus 2 tablespoons packed brown sugar

⅓ cup granulated sugar

2 large eggs

¼ cup buttermilk

1 teaspoon pure vanilla extract

For the red velvet cake:

1 cup plus 2 tablespoons all-purpose flour

¾ teaspoon baking soda

½ teaspoon salt

3 tablespoons unsweetened cocoa powder

2 tablespoons red food coloring

¼ cup (½ stick) unsalted butter, at room temperature

¾ cup granulated sugar

1 large egg

½ teaspoon pure vanilla extract

½ cup buttermilk

1½ teaspoons white vinegar

Place oven racks in the center and upper third of the oven and preheat to 350 degrees F. Grease and flour two 8– or 9-inch round cake pans and set aside.

To make the chocolate cake: in a medium bowl, whisk together flour, baking soda, and salt. Set aside.

Whisk together coffee and cocoa. Set aside.

In the bowl of a stand mixer fitted with a paddle attachment, beat together butter, brown sugar, and granulated sugar. Beat until fluffy, 3 to 5 minutes. Add eggs one at a time, beating for 1 minute between each addition. Stop the mixer and scrape down the bowl as necessary. Add the coffee mixture and vanilla to the butter mixture and beat on medium-high speed for 1 minute, until thoroughly combined.

With the mixer on low, add the flour mixture and buttermilk. Beat until almost entirely combined. Remove the bowl from the mixer, and finish mixing the batter with a spatula. Set aside.

To make the red velvet cake: in a medium bowl, whisk together flour, baking soda, and salt. Set aside.

In a small bowl, mix together cocoa and red food coloring. Set aside.

In the bowl of an electric stand mixer fitted with a paddle attachment, beat butter and sugar until light and fluffy, 3 to 5 minutes. Add the egg, beating at medium speed for 1 minute. Add the cocoa mixture along with the vanilla, and beat until completely blended. Stop the mixer and use a spatula to scrape down the bowl as needed.

With the mixer on low speed, add half of the flour mixture and half of the buttermilk to the butter mixture. When almost completely incorporated, add the remaining flour and buttermilk to the batter. Beat on low speed until almost entirely incorporated. Remove the bowl from the mixer, add the vinegar, and finish combining the batter with a spatula.

When batter is well combined, divide the red velvet cake batter between the prepared pans. Top each with the chocolate cake batter by dividing that batter between pans. Use a butter knife to gently swirl the 2 cake batters together. This won't take more than a few strokes in each pan; you want each batter to remain fairly distinct and not get too muddled.

Bake cakes on the center and upper oven racks for 15 minutes. Switch the cake pans from the bottom to the top and vice versa and bake for another 15 to 20 minutes, until a skewer inserted in the center of the cakes comes out clean.

Remove from the oven and let cakes cool in the pan for 10 minutes before inverting onto wire racks to cool completely.

Once cool, frost with The Best Chocolate Buttercream Frosting (p. 133). Refrigerate for 30 minutes to let the frosting set slightly before serving. Cake will last, well wrapped, in the fridge for 5 days.

buttermilk skillet cake with walnut praline topping

makes one 8- or 9-inch cake

I became a baker so I could eat cakes like this. This cake doesn't make a spectacle or need a lot of attention. It's a tender buttermilk cake made in a simple cast-iron skillet. But pour warm walnut praline topping over it, and I guarantee that you might consider a career change. This cake is just that good.

For the cake:

1½ cups all-purpose flour

¾ teaspoon baking powder

¼ teaspoon baking soda

¾ teaspoon salt

6 tablespoons (¾ stick)
    unsalted butter, softened

1 cup granulated sugar

1 large egg

1 large egg yolk

2 teaspoons pure vanilla extract

¾ cup buttermilk

For the praline topping:

¾ cup packed brown sugar

½ cup (1 stick) unsalted butter

¼ cup heavy cream

Generous pinch of salt

1 teaspoon pure vanilla extract

1 cup coarsely chopped walnuts

Place a rack in the upper third of the oven and preheat to 375 degrees F. Grease and flour the bottom and sides of an 8-inch ovenproof pan (preferably a cast-iron skillet) and set aside. A 9-inch cake pan will also work.

To make the cake: in a medium bowl, whisk together flour, baking powder, baking soda, and salt. Set aside.

In the bowl of an electric stand mixer fitted with a paddle attachment, beat butter and sugar until well incorporated and lighter in color, about 3 minutes. Add egg and yolk, beating for 1 minute between each addition. Beat in the vanilla.

With the mixer on low, add half of the flour mixture. Add the buttermilk and when flour is just combined with the butter mixture, add the remaining flour. Beat on low speed until almost all of the flour has disappeared. Remove the bowl from the mixer and finish incorporating ingredients with a spatula. Spoon batter into prepared pan and spread evenly. Bake for about 30 minutes or until a skewer inserted in the center of the cake comes out clean.

While the cake bakes, make the praline topping: in a medium saucepan, combine brown sugar, butter, cream, and salt over medium heat. Bring the mixture to a soft boil for 3 minutes. Remove from the heat and add vanilla and nuts. Stir.

Mixture may seem too loose for the cake, but let it sit in the pan for 20 minutes. It'll firm up. After the mixture has rested for 20 minutes, and the cake has been baked and removed from the oven, pour the praline mixture over the warm cake. If you baked this cake in a cake pan instead of cast iron, remove the cake from the pan, place on a cake plate, and pour topping over cake. Spread evenly. Serve immediately or at room temperature.

Cake will last, well wrapped, at room temperature for up to 4 days.

zucchini cream cheese pound cake

makes one Bundt cake

You know that special flavor a cake takes on when it is made by the hands of your grandmother? This cake totally has the flavor! It's uncanny! This pound cake is dense but subtle. Zucchini adds moisture, and works well with the touch of cinnamon. The cream cheese in the cake and in the frosting adds a richness and a little tang. While it is subtle and slightly understated, each bite brings a certain indescribable comfort.

3 cups all-purpose flour	2 teaspoons ground cinnamon	2 teaspoons pure vanilla extract
1 teaspoon baking soda	8 ounces cream cheese, softened	1 cup (2 sticks) unsalted butter,
½ teaspoon baking powder	2 cups granulated sugar	melted and cooled
1 teaspoon salt	3 large eggs	2 cups shredded zucchini

Place a rack in the upper third of the oven and preheat to 350 degrees F. Grease and flour a 12-cup Bundt pan and set aside.

In a medium bowl, whisk together flour, baking soda, baking powder, salt, and cinnamon. Set aside.

In the bowl of an electric stand mixer, beat cream cheese and sugar on medium speed until well incorporated, about 2 minutes. Add eggs, one at a time, beating for 1 minute between each addition, then add vanilla. With the mixer on low speed, pour in the melted butter and increase speed to medium-high to beat until velvety smooth, about 3 minutes.

Reduce mixer speed to low and add flour mixture, all at once, to the mixture. Beat until just incorporated. Remove the bowl from the mixer and use a spatula to fold in the zucchini, and incorporate the rest of the flour. The batter will be thick, not pourable.

Spoon batter into prepared pan and bake for 45 to 50 minutes, until a skewer inserted into the center comes out clean. Remove cake from oven and allow to cool in the pan for 20 minutes before inverting onto a wire rack to cool completely.

When completely cooled, frost the entire cake with Brown Sugar Cream Cheese Frosting (p. 137).

banana rum cake with brown butter frosting

makes one 2-layer 8- or 9-inch round cake

Raise your hand if you like booze in your cake! I totally have my hand raised. This is the cake that I would make every single day if I were a Southern housewife. I'd also wear big hats, sip mint drinks from straws, and call my husband "Sugar." I'm not a Southern housewife, so I only make this cake a few times a year. That's a shame, really.

This cake is full of all sorts of goodness. Bananas and buttermilk contribute both flavor and moistness, rum makes it festive, and Brown Butter Frosting results in an over-the-top sensation. Wear a big hat if you've got one.

For the cake:

3 cups all-purpose flour

2¼ teaspoons baking powder

¾ teaspoon baking soda

1 teaspoon salt

1½ teaspoons ground cinnamon

½ teaspoon freshly grated nutmeg

¾ cup (1½ sticks) unsalted butter, at room temperature

1¾ cups packed brown sugar

2¼ cups mashed bananas (about 4 medium)

3 tablespoons rum

3 large eggs

½ cup plus 2 tablespoons buttermilk

½ cup chopped pecans

For the brown butter frosting:

¾ cup (1½ sticks) salted butter

3 cups powdered sugar, sifted

1 tablespoon pure vanilla extract

1 tablespoon rum

½ cup heavy cream

Place a rack in the center and upper third of the oven, and preheat to 350 degrees F. Grease and flour two 8- or 9-inch round cake pans. Set aside.

To make the cake: in a medium bowl, whisk together flour, baking powder, baking soda, salt, cinnamon, and nutmeg. Set aside.

In the bowl of an electric stand mixer fitted with a paddle attachment, cream together butter and brown sugar. Mix on medium speed for 3 minutes, until light and fluffy. Add mashed bananas and rum and blend for another minute, until thoroughly combined. Add the eggs one at a time, beating for 1 minute between each addition.

With the mixer on low speed, add half of the flour mixture to the butter mixture. Add the buttermilk and beat on low until the mixture just begins to come together. Add the remaining flour mixture and beat until the mixture is almost entirely incorporated. Remove the bowl from the mixer and finish blending the ingredients with a spatula. Fold in the pecans.

Divide the batter between the cake pans. Bake for 30 minutes on alternating racks, switching the cakes halfway through

baking. When a cake tester inserted in the center comes out clean, remove the cakes from the oven. Let cakes rest in the pan for 20 minutes before inverting onto a wire rack to cool completely before frosting.

To make the brown butter frosting: in a medium saucepan over medium heat, melt butter until browned in color and nutty in fragrance. Pour browned butter into a small bowl to cool. The browned bits will add color and character to the frosting.

In the bowl of an electric stand mixer fitted with a paddle attachment, add powdered sugar, turn mixer on low, and add browned butter in a stream. Increase speed to medium, and add vanilla and rum. Beat for 2 minutes. Reduce speed to low, and slowly add cream. Increase speed to medium and beat until smooth and creamy. If mixture is too thick, add a touch of cream. If mixture is too thin, add a touch more powdered sugar. Spread between the layers and on top and sides of cooled cake.

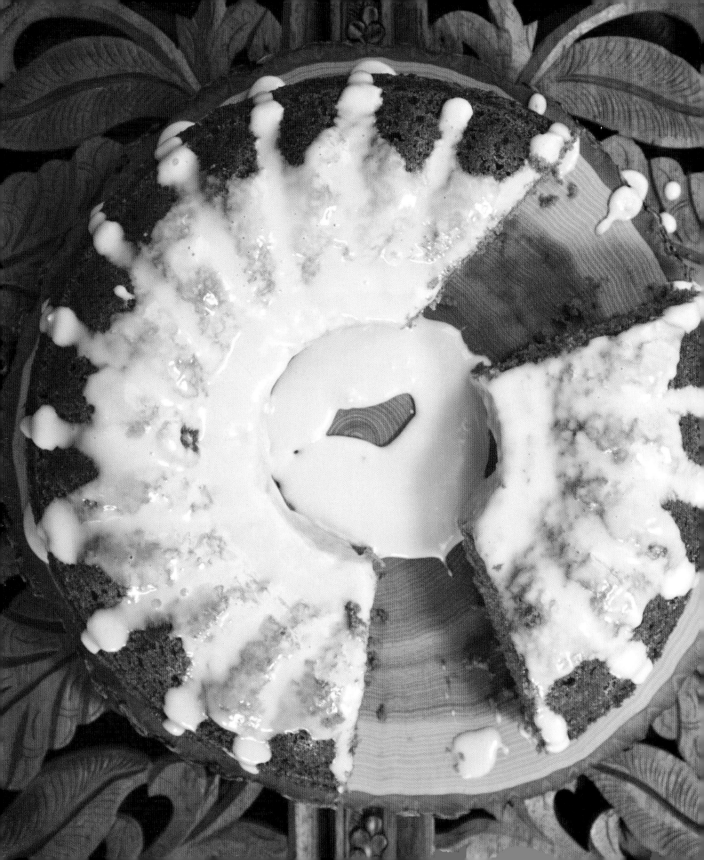

araby spice cake with lemon glaze

makes one 9-inch round cake

This recipe is older than dirt. Okay, maybe not dirt, but this recipe is significantly older than me by several generations. My blind aunt made a version of this cake for every holiday or birthday celebration. The cake was always lopsided and curiously frosted, but if I tried baking a cake while blindfolded, I'm fairly certain I wouldn't even be able to locate my kitchen.

Essentially, this is a spice cake with cocoa powder and lemon zest. Does that sound crazy? The cake doesn't have a strong chocolate or lemon taste, but the cocoa and citrus marry with the spices to create an enticing cake. It's unique and lovely and tastes of generations of loving inspiration.

For the cake:

2 cups all-purpose flour

1 teaspoon baking powder

¼ teaspoon baking soda

½ teaspoon salt

3 tablespoons unsweetened
   cocoa powder

¾ cup (1½ sticks) unsalted butter,
   at room temperature

1½ cups granulated sugar

1 teaspoon ground cinnamon

½ teaspoon ground cloves

¼ teaspoon ground allspice

1 teaspoon lemon zest

3 large eggs

¾ cup buttermilk

For the glaze:

2 cups powdered sugar, sifted

3 tablespoons fresh lemon juice

1 to 2 tablespoons milk

Place a rack in the upper third of the oven and preheat to 350 degrees F. Grease and flour a 9-inch round cake pan or spray generously with nonstick cooking spray.

To make the cake: in a medium bowl, whisk together flour, baking powder, baking soda, salt and cocoa powder. Set aside.

In the bowl of an electric stand mixer fitted with a paddle attachment, blend together butter, sugar, cinnamon, cloves, allspice, and lemon zest. Beat until light and fluffy, 3 to 5 minutes. Reduce mixer speed to low and beat in eggs, one at a time, beating for about 1 minute between each addition. Stop the mixer occasionally to scrape down the sides of the bowl with a spatula. This will ensure that everything gets mixed evenly.

Add half of the flour mixture to the butter mixture. With the mixer on low speed, add half of the buttermilk. Beat until just combined. Add the remaining flour mixture and buttermilk, and beat until combined—no more than 1 minute. Incorporate any remaining unmixed flour with a spatula.

Spoon batter into prepared pan, and bake for 30 to 40 minutes, until a cake tester inserted in the center comes out clean. Let cool in the pan for 10 minutes before inverting onto a cooling rack to cool completely.

To make the glaze: whisk together powdered sugar, lemon juice, and milk. Drizzle the glaze over the cooled cake, and let sit for 20 minutes before serving with coffee or tea. Cake will last, well wrapped, at room temperature for up to 4 days.

vegan chocolate avocado cupcakes with vegan chocolate buttercream

makes 12 to 14 cupcakes

This is the part of our baking journey that will make you raise your eyebrows at me. Yes, this fine chocolate cake has avocado in it. Avocados are so rich and creamy that I like to consider them the vegetable equivalent of butter. This vegan cake recipe uses both oil and avocado to create a moist, tender, and sturdy crumb. Combine the cake with vegan chocolate frosting, and you've got quite a treat. You won't have to tell a soul that there's avocado in the cake, unless of course, you want to brag.

You can double this cake and frosting recipe to make one 2-layer 8- or 9-inch cake.

For the cupcakes:
1½ cups all-purpose flour
¼ cup unsweetened cocoa powder
¼ teaspoon salt
1 teaspoon baking powder
1 teaspoon baking soda
1 cup granulated sugar
2 tablespoons vegetable oil

¼ cup mashed ripe avocado
1 cup water
1 tablespoon white vinegar
1 teaspoon pure vanilla extract
For the vegan chocolate buttercream:
¾ cup Earth Balance butter
    (or any vegan butter in sticks),
    at room temperature

2 tablespoons unsweetened
    cocoa powder
2 to 2½ cups powdered sugar
1 teaspoon pure vanilla extract
1 to 2 tablespoons soy milk

Place rack in the upper third of the oven, and preheat oven to 350 degrees F. Line a cupcake pan with foil or paper liners. Set aside.

To make the cupcakes: in a medium bowl, whisk together flour, cocoa powder, salt, baking powder, and baking soda. Set aside.

In a large bowl, whisk together sugar, oil, avocado, water, vinegar, and vanilla. Add the flour mixture to the avocado mixture and fold with a spatula until well combined. You can even use a whisk to ensure that everything is well mixed.

The batter is so loose that it's easiest to place the batter in a liquid measuring cup and pour into paper liners. Fill the cupcake liners until about two-thirds full. Place the pan in the upper third of the oven. Bake for 18 to 20 minutes or until a skewer inserted into the center of the cupcake comes out clean. Let the cupcakes cool in the pan for 10 minutes before transferring onto wire racks to cool completely.

To make the vegan chocolate buttercream: place the butter in the bowl of an electric stand mixer fitted with a paddle attachment. Beat the butter on medium speed until soft and pliable. Stop the mixer, scrape down the bowl, and add the

cocoa powder and sugar. Turn mixer on low to slowly incorporate. Add the vanilla and soy milk. Increase the mixer speed to medium or medium-high and beat the mixture until frosting is soft and fluffy.

Spoon frosting on top of cupcakes and smooth with a butter knife. Decorate with sprinkles if desired. Store frosted cupcakes, well wrapped, in the refrigerator for up to 4 days.

espresso granita with sweet lemon cream

makes about 2½ cups granita

My favorite thing about having fancy espresso in dainty white cups is the little curl of lemon zest that accompanies the hot coffee. Lemon and coffee? This dessert is a unique way to incorporate those two flavors. Lemon helps to take the hard acidity out of the espresso. It's really a divine trick. The espresso granita is bold and icy. The whipped cream is fluffy, fragrant, and sweet. The pairing is pretty dang classy. Just look at you, being all fancy.

For the granita:

2½ cups water

Heaping ⅓ cup freshly ground espresso

1½ tablespoons granulated sugar

3 teaspoons instant espresso powder (optional)

For the lemon cream:

3 tablespoons granulated sugar

1 teaspoon lemon zest

1½ cups heavy cream

To make the granita: bring water to boil and pour over freshly ground coffee in a French press. If you don't have a French press, just make 2½ cups of strong coffee in your coffeemaker. Pour hot coffee into a shallow freezer-friendly dish and stir in sugar and espresso powder (if using). I don't like to use anything metal because wet fingers stick to the pan.

Allow coffee to rest in the freezer for an hour. After an hour, stir mixture with a fork. Allow to rest for another hour, stir once again with a fork. Allow to rest for 30 minutes, then stir again with a fork. The mixture will begin to freeze, and stirring ensures that coffee flakes and flecks are created instead of a solid block of coffee ice. After 3 to 4 hours, granita will be frozen and flaky. Once it's flaked, it can rest in the freezer until ready to serve.

To make the lemon cream: place sugar on a clean cutting board or counter surface. With the back of a spoon or a bench knife, press the lemon zest into the sugar for about 3 minutes. The coarse sugar will release the essential oils from the zest, creating a fragrant flavored sugar.

In the bowl of an electric stand mixer fitted with a whisk attachment, beat cream for 1 minute. Add the scented sugar and whisk until soft whipped cream peaks form.

Serve cream alongside coffee granita in small dishes. Granita will last up to 3 days in the freezer. Perfect for a little afternoon snack.

coffee vanilla ice cream pie

makes one 9-inch pie

Why serve ice cream next to pie when you can serve ice cream *as* pie? This recipe has a sweet and toothsome meringue crust, and is filled with coffee and vanilla ice cream. I think these ice cream flavors are delicate and sophisticated, but if you want to throw in some chocolate and strawberry, I'm sure no one would be disappointed by your choices. The inspiration for this pie came from *The Pioneer Woman*. I wonder if everything tastes better on the prairie. It's entirely possible.

For the crust:

¼ cup egg whites (from 2 eggs)

¼ teaspoon salt

¼ cup granulated sugar

⅔ cup crumbled vanilla wafers

½ cup finely chopped pecans
   or walnuts

½ teaspoon orange zest

For the filling:

1 pint coffee ice cream

1 pint vanilla ice cream

For the topping:

1½ cups heavy cream

¼ cup powdered sugar

1 teaspoon pure vanilla extract

Place a rack in the center of the oven and preheat to 350 degrees F.

To make the crust: in the bowl of an electric stand mixer fitted with a whisk attachment, beat egg whites until foamy. Add salt and gradually add sugar. Beat on high until stiff and glossy. Remove bowl from the mixer and fold in vanilla wafers, pecans, and orange zest. Pour the mixture into a 9-inch pie pan, and spread across the bottom and the sides of the pan. Bake for 15 to 20 minutes or until golden brown. Keep an eye on this crust—it burns quickly. Remove from the oven and allow to cool completely before filling with ice cream.

To make the filling: while cake is cooling, remove ice cream from the freezer. To soften the ice cream, just before filling the pie, remove each ice cream from pint container and place in separate medium bowls. Stir each ice cream with a spatula until soft and pliable.

When crust is completely cooled, fill the bottom and sides of the pie crust with vanilla ice cream. Next, add the coffee ice cream. Cover the pie with foil or plastic wrap and freeze until very firm.

To make the topping: when ready to serve pie, whip cream, sugar, and vanilla in the bowl of an electric stand mixer until soft and fluffy. Spread on top of the pie and slice pie into large wedges.

NOTE: This pie would be extra super delicious if you add coarsely chopped chocolate-covered espresso beans to the coffee ice cream. Yum!

simple vanilla cupcakes

makes 1 dozen cupcakes

Sometimes I want to skip the chocolate and the chunks and the fruit and the spices. Sometimes I just want vanilla, pure and simple. These cupcakes are just the treat for such occasions. Golden yellow, with a dense but surprisingly light cake crumb, these cupcakes remind me of my ninth birthday party. I got a goldfish, and I got to run through the sprinklers in the backyard. I had everything I ever wanted, including this cake. You can double the recipe and make one 2-layer 8- or 9-inch cake.

1⅓ cups all-purpose flour
¾ teaspoon baking powder
¼ teaspoon salt

½ cup (1 stick) unsalted butter, softened
1 cup granulated sugar
2 large eggs

2 teaspoons pure vanilla extract
½ vanilla bean, seeds scraped out
½ cup whole milk

Place a rack in the upper third of the oven and preheat to 350 degrees F. Line a 12-cup cupcake pan with paper or foil liners and set aside.

In a medium bowl, whisk together flour, baking powder, and salt. Set aside.

In the bowl of an electric stand mixer fitted with a paddle attachment, cream butter and sugar until light and fluffy, 3 to 5 minutes. Add eggs one at a time, beating for 1 minute after each addition. Beat in the vanilla extract and vanilla bean seeds until well incorporated.

Add half of the flour mixture and beat on low speed until almost incorporated. Add the milk. Blend. Add the rest of the flour mixture and beat until almost incorporated. Remove the bowl from the mixer, and finish incorporating the ingredients with a spatula.

Divide the batter between the cupcake liners. Bake for 20 to 25 minutes, until golden brown and a skewer inserted in the center of the cupcakes comes out clean.

Remove from the oven and let rest in the pan for 10 minutes before removing to a wire rack to cool completely.

Frost with The Best Chocolate Buttercream Frosting (p. 133), Chocolate Cream Cheese Frosting (p. 139), or Vanilla Bean Buttercream Frosting (p. 143).

pineapple malted milkshake

makes one 3-cup milkshake

We have a Saturday-night tradition in my family. It involves a long car ride, spicy Mexican food, almost painful amounts of chips and guacamole, and finishes with a trip to the local ice cream shop for pineapple malted milkshakes. Then, my father invariably jokes about driving off without either me or my sister in the car, and we have to rush back to the car, malts in hand, so as not to be left behind. It's all in good fun…I think.

1 cup whole or low-fat milk

2 cups vanilla ice cream

3 tablespoons malted milk powder

½ teaspoon pure vanilla extract

1 cup fresh pineapple chunks (see note)

NOTE: if you're using canned pineapple, try ⅓ cup crushed pineapple, drained of most of the juice.

In a blender combine milk, ice cream, malted milk powder, vanilla, and pineapple. Blend on high until smooth, thick, and creamy. Pour into a tall glass and enjoy immediately.

strawberry cookie dough ice cream

makes 1 quart

Are you one of those people who will eat every last chunk of candy or cookie dough from the ice cream pint, then return the deflated melty ice cream remains to the freezer, only to wholeheartedly deny such ice cream scavenging when confronted? Then you are an ice cream picker! I am too. My ice cream picking is a problem, so I created a solution. More chunks! I've created an ice cream with so much chunky goodness that you'll have a hard time picking through it. There are chunks in every bite. Pickers, meet your match.

For the cookie dough:
1 cup plus 2 tablespoons
    all-purpose flour
½ teaspoon baking soda
¾ teaspoon salt
½ cup (1 stick) unsalted butter,
    softened
½ cup packed brown sugar

⅓ cup granulated sugar
1 teaspoon pure vanilla extract
3 tablespoons milk
1 cup (6 ounces) semisweet
    chocolate chips
For the ice cream:
¾ cup granulated sugar
5 large egg yolks

Pinch of salt
2 cups whole milk
2 tablespoons honey
2 teaspoons pure vanilla extract
1 cup heavy cream
1 cup frozen strawberries,
    partially thawed

To make the cookie dough: in a medium bowl, whisk together flour, baking soda, and salt. Set aside.

In the bowl of an electric stand mixer, cream together butter, brown sugar, and granulated sugar until light and fluffy, 3 to 5 minutes. Blend in the vanilla and milk. With the mixer on low speed, add the flour mixture. Blend until mixture almost comes together but flour is still visible. Turn off the mixer and remove the bowl from the stand. Add chocolate chips and finish blending the mixture with a spatula.

Spoon the dough onto a sheet of plastic wrap. Wrap into a log and refrigerate while you prepare the ice cream.

To make the ice cream: whisk together sugar, egg yolks, and salt in a medium bowl. Whisk until thick and pale. Set aside.

In a medium saucepan, warm milk and honey until almost boiling. Gradually pour the warm milk into the egg yolk mixture in a steady stream. Be sure to whisk constantly so the egg yolks don't get cooked. Return the milk and egg mixture to the saucepan and cook over medium-low heat, stirring often with a spatula. Cook until the mixture is thickened and the custard holds a line across the back of the spatula. This usually takes about 8 minutes. You'll be able to smell the eggs cooking just as the custard is finished cooking.

Pour mixture over a fine-mesh strainer into a medium bowl. This will ensure that no cooked egg bits get into the custard.

Stir in the vanilla, and cream. Place a piece of plastic wrap directly over the custard and place in the fridge to chill before churning.

While the custard cools, roll chilled cookie dough into 50 small marble-sized balls. Place on a small cookie sheet and store in the freezer until ready to incorporate into ice cream. Coarsely chop the strawberries, place in a bowl, and store in the refrigerator.

When ice cream custard is cool (this takes several hours), churn according to ice cream maker instructions. Once the ice cream is almost completely churned, add the strawberries to the ice cream machine. Churn until well incorporated and pale pink. Transfer ice cream to a freezer-friendly container, fold in the dough balls, and freeze until more solid before serving.

Ice cream will last for up to 5 days in the freezer.

the best chocolate buttercream frosting

makes enough to frost one 2-layer 8- or 9-inch cake or 24 cupcakes

I'm here to make you some promises. This is the best buttercream frosting I've ever made. This will be the best buttercream frosting you'll ever make. The secret ingredient is Ovaltine, the chocolate malted powder. When mixed with heavy cream, Ovaltine adds a velvety smooth texture to the buttercream, making it soft and creamy but not overly sweet. On cakes or cupcakes, this frosting is glossy good. This recipe is inspired by Delilah Bakery.

¾ cup (1½ sticks) unsalted butter,
    at room temperature
½ cup unsweetened cocoa powder

½ teaspoon salt
2½ to 3 cups powdered sugar, sifted
2 tablespoons milk

1 teaspoon vanilla extract
Scant ½ cup heavy cream
⅓ cup Ovaltine powder

In the bowl of an electric stand mixer fitted with a paddle attachment, cream together butter, cocoa powder, and salt. Mixture will be very thick, but cream for about 3 minutes on medium speed.

    Turn off the mixer, scrape down the sides of the bowl and add the 2½ cups powdered sugar. Turn the mixer on low to incorporate the sugar while adding the milk and vanilla. As the sugar incorporates, gradually increase the mixer speed to medium-high. Stop the mixer and scrape down the sides of the bowl as necessary. Beat until smooth.

    In a 1-cup measure, stir together cream and Ovaltine. Turn the mixer to medium, and pour the cream in a slow and steady stream until the frosting reaches your desired consistency: smooth, creamy, and spreadable. Add more powdered sugar to adjust consistency. Spread or pipe frosting onto cooled cakes or cupcakes.

    Frosting will last, well wrapped, in the refrigerator for up to 5 days.

NOTE: Putting the frosting in the fridge for about 30 minutes makes it harden just a little and makes it easier to spread as a frosting.

cream cheese frosting: the basics

Listen, I'm a huge fan of cream cheese frosting. The delectable mixture of butter, cream cheese, and sugar is spreadable and silky smooth. What more do you want from life? There is an ugly side to cream cheese frosting. Have you ever put your last block of cream cheese and last few sticks of butter into the mixer, hoping for perfect frosting, only to emerge with a curdled mess? It's the pits. I never want that to happen to you, so here are some frosting tips, from someone who has learned the hard way.

Cream cheese frosting is a simple mix of three ingredients. What could possibly go wrong? Temperatures. In order to be properly incorporated into frosting, cream cheese needs to be completely softened. No, don't even think of microwaving. This will break down the cream cheese too much. Just leave the cream cheese out on the counter until it is perfectly room temperature.

Butter is a different story altogether. The butter needs to be softened, but leaving the but-

ter out overnight would be a disaster. I leave my butter on the counter for 2 to 3 hours before I make the frosting. This ensures that the butter is soft, but still has a slight chill to it and easily holds its cube shape. If the butter is too soft, the water in the butter will be easily separated from the fat in the butter, and that's what creates the curdling.

There's more! The way in which you incorporate the fats is also important. Start with the cream cheese in the bowl of an electric stand mixer. Beat the cream cheese, alone, for 1 minute. Stop the mixer and add the softened (but not mushy) butter. Beat the two fats together on medium speed for another minute. Stopping the mixer occasionally to scrape down the sides of the bowl is a nice touch, and will ensure that everything is thoroughly mixed. Once your fats have joined forces, you're nearly home free! Just add your sugars, any flavoring or zest, and beat until smooth and fluffy.

Breathe a sigh of relief, and taste a big dollop of your creation. Use your finger; I won't tell a soul.

cream cheese frosting

makes enough to frost one 2-layer 8- or 9-inch cake or 24 cupcakes

A classic frosting, delicious on Kitchen Sink Carrot Cake (p. 109) and Banana Rum Cake (p. 116).

8 ounces cream cheese, softened
½ cup (1 stick) unsalted butter,
    softened
Pinch of salt

2 cups powdered sugar, sifted
2 teaspoons pure vanilla extract
Variations:
1 vanilla bean

½ cup chocolate hazelnut spread
1 tablespoon lemon juice
    plus 2 teaspoons lemon zest

Place cream cheese in the bowl of an electric stand mixer fitted with a paddle attachment. Beat the cream cheese for about 1 minute, ensuring that it is soft and pliable. Stop the mixer and use a spatula to scrape down the sides of the bowl. Add the butter to the bowl. Beat the butter and cream cheese on medium speed for 1 minute, until thoroughly combined.

If adding any extra ingredients like a scraped vanilla bean, chocolate hazelnut spread, or lemon, do so after the cream cheese and butter have been mixed.

Turn the mixer on low and add the salt and powdered sugar followed by the vanilla extract. Beat until almost incorporated.

Stop the mixer and scrape down the sides and the bottom of the bowl. Beat on medium speed until all of the powdered sugar has disappeared and mixture is velvety soft.

Use immediately by spreading on a layer cake or cupcakes. If not using immediately, store in an airtight container in the refrigerator and bring to room temperature before spreading on cakes. Frosting will last, in an airtight container, in the refrigerator for up to 7 days.

brown sugar cream cheese frosting

makes enough to frost one 2-layer 8- or 9-inch cake or 24 cupcakes

Rich and delicious. This frosting is beautiful on Pumpkin Bundt Cake (p. 105) or Zucchini Cream Cheese Pound Cake (p. 114).

8 ounces cream cheese, softened

½ cup (1 stick) unsalted butter, softened

⅓ cup packed brown sugar

1 teaspoon molasses

Pinch of salt

1¾ cups powdered sugar, sifted

2 teaspoons pure vanilla extract

Place cream cheese in the bowl of an electric stand mixer fitted with a paddle attachment. Beat the cream cheese for about 1 minute, ensuring that it is soft and pliable. Stop the mixer and use a spatula to scrape down the sides of the bowl. Add the softened butter to the bowl. Beat the butter and cream cheese on medium speed for 1 minute, until thoroughly combined.

Add brown sugar and molasses to the cream cheese and butter, and beat on medium speed for 30 seconds. Turn the mixer on low and add the salt and powdered sugar followed by the vanilla. Beat until almost incorporated. Stop the mixer and scrape down the sides and the bottom of the bowl. Beat on medium speed until all of the powdered sugar has disappeared and mixture is velvety soft.

Use immediately by spreading on a layer cake or cupcakes. If not using immediately, store in an airtight container in the refrigerator and bring to room temperature before spreading on cakes. Frosting will last, in an airtight container, in the refrigerator for up to 7 days.

chocolate cream cheese frosting

makes enough to frost one 2-layer 8- or 9-inch cake or 24 cupcakes

Cocoa and cream cheese are a match made in heaven. This frosting is lovely on Peanut Butter Birthday Cake (p. 106) or the Red Velvet Marble Cake (p. 110).

8 ounces cream cheese, softened
½ cup (1 stick) unsalted butter, softened

¼ cup unsweetened cocoa powder
Pinch of salt
2 cups powdered sugar, sifted

2 teaspoons pure vanilla extract
1 teaspoon milk

Place cream cheese in the bowl of an electric stand mixer fitted with a paddle attachment. Beat the cream cheese for about 1 minute, ensuring that it is soft and pliable. Stop the mixer and use a spatula to scrape down the sides of the bowl. Add the butter to the bowl. Beat the butter and cream cheese on medium speed for 1 minute until thoroughly combined.

Add cocoa powder and beat for 30 seconds on medium speed, until incorporated. Turn the mixer on low and add the salt and powdered sugar followed by the vanilla extract and milk. Beat until almost incorporated.

Stop the mixer and scrape down the sides and the bottom of the bowl. Beat on medium speed until all of the powdered sugar has disappeared and mixture is velvety soft.

Use immediately by spreading on a layer cake or cupcakes. If not using immediately, store in an airtight container in the refrigerator and bring to room temperature before spreading on cakes. Frosting will last, in an airtight container, in the refrigerator for up to 7 days.

peanut butter cream cheese frosting

makes enough to frost one 2-layer 8- or 9-inch cake or 24 cupcakes

Peanut butter adds a touch of saltiness to tangy cream cheese frosting. This frosting is perfectly paired with Peanut Butter Birthday Cake (p. 106) and Simple Vanilla Cupcakes (p. 127).

8 ounces cream cheese, softened
½ cup (1 stick) unsalted butter, softened

⅓ cup plus 2 tablespoons smooth peanut butter
Pinch of salt

2 cups powdered sugar, sifted
2 teaspoons pure vanilla extract

Place cream cheese in the bowl of an electric stand mixer fitted with a paddle attachment. Beat the cream cheese for about 1 minute, ensuring that it is soft and pliable. Stop the mixer and use a spatula to scrape down the sides of the bowl. Add the butter to the bowl. Beat the butter and cream cheese on medium speed for 1 minute until thoroughly combined.

Add ⅓ cup of the peanut butter to the cream cheese mixture. Beat for 30 seconds on medium speed, until well combined. Turn the mixer on low and add the salt and powdered sugar followed by the vanilla. Beat until almost incorporated. Stop the mixer and scrape down the sides and the bottom of the bowl. Beat on medium speed until all of the powdered sugar has disappeared and mixture is velvety soft.

If using immediately, dollop 2 tablespoons of peanut butter into the finished cream cheese and fold in with a spatula. Don't completely mix, leave streaks of peanut butter throughout the frosting. Use immediately to frost cakes or cupcakes.

If storing for later use, spoon frosting into an airtight container, add peanut butter, swirl into the frosting and store in the fridge until ready to use. Bring the frosting to room temperature before frosting a cake or cupcakes.

Frosting will last, in an airtight container, in the refrigerator for up to 7 days.

vanilla bean buttercream frosting

makes enough to frost one 2-layer 8- or 9-inch cake or 24 cupcakes

This classic American frosting is super thick and creamy. This is the perfect frosting to tint with color and swirl on cupcakes.

1 cup (2 sticks) unsalted butter, softened but still holding its shape
4 to 5 cups powdered sugar, sifted
2 tablespoons milk
1 vanilla bean, seeds scraped (or 1 tablespoon pure vanilla extract)
Pinch of salt

In the bowl of an electric stand mixer fitted with a paddle attachment, beat butter for 2 minutes, until light and fluffy.

Scrape the butter from the sides of the bowl and add 3 cups of the powdered sugar. Beat on low, increasing to medium speed as the mixture combines. Add milk and vanilla bean or extract. Beat on high for 1 minute.

Stop the mixer, scrape down the sides of the bowl, and add 1 more cup powdered sugar. Beat on medium speed until light and fluffy. If you'd like a thicker frosting, add up to a cup more powdered sugar, beating well. Frost completely cooked cakes or cupcakes.

Frosting will last, in an airtight container, for 10 days in the refrigerator.

5

i think i just ate chocolate for dinner

don't worry, your secret is safe with me.

I'm a single girl. That means that I don't have to feed anyone but myself come dinnertime. Sure, sometimes that fact is a little sad, but I'm a girl who embraces single-serving meals. That means that I can have chocolate and popcorn for dinner.

I'm totally okay with having chocolate for dinner. Not all nights, but some for sure. I just have to make sure that when the time comes to actually cook for a date, I know how to make something other than The Perfect Cup of Hot Chocolate and Dark Chocolate Sorbet.

the perfect cup of hot chocolate

makes 2 cups

Solo hot chocolate has its charm, but there's something extra comforting about curling up on a couch with a hunky guy and a cup of warm, milky chocolate. This recipe calls for two sorts of chocolate chips. I always seem to have open, random bags of chocolate chips in my pantry, and this is a great way to use them up. Cheers!

¼ cup semisweet chocolate chips

2 heaping tablespoons
   white chocolate chips

2 cups milk (any fat content)

½ teaspoon instant coffee powder
   (optional, but delicious)

Pinch of salt

Pour about 2 inches of water into a medium saucepan and place over medium heat. Place dark and white chocolate chips in a heatproof bowl. When the water has come to a simmer, place the bowl of water on top but not touching the simmering water. Stir until chocolate is melted.

   Meanwhile, in a small saucepan, heat milk until almost boiling. Whisk the melted chocolate, coffee powder, and salt into the heating milk and whisk until smooth and incorporated.

   Pour into 2 cups and enjoy with marshmallows. Hot chocolate is best served immediately.

mommom's chocolate bourbon-spiked banana bread

makes one 8x4-inch or 9x5-inch loaf

Dear Mommom,

I love your banana bread. It's moist and uncomplicated, full of banana bits and supreme comfort. I've enjoyed your banana bread for as long as I can remember. Dad makes a low-fat version of your banana bread but, come on! I just can't get behind that. Your recipe reigns supreme.

Just one thing though, I added chocolate and bourbon to your classic. What can I say—I'm young and reckless.

Love,
Your Dear and Darling Granddaughter

2 cups all-purpose flour

3 teaspoons baking powder

½ teaspoon salt

½ cup (1 stick) unsalted butter, softened

1 cup granulated sugar

2 large eggs

1½ cups mashed ripe bananas (about 3)

1 teaspoon lemon juice

3 tablespoons bourbon

1 cup coarsely chopped walnuts

1 cup (6 ounces) semisweet chocolate chips

Place a rack in the center of the oven and preheat to 350 degrees F. Grease and flour an 8x4- or 9x5-inch loaf pan. Set aside.

In a medium bowl, sift together flour, baking powder, and salt.

In the bowl of an electric stand mixer fitted with a paddle attachment, beat butter and sugar until light and fluffy, 3 to 5 minutes.

Add eggs one at a time, beating for 1 minute between each addition. Stop the mixer, scrape down the sides of the bowl and add bananas, lemon juice, and bourbon. Beat until well incorporated.

Turn the mixer to low and add the flour mixture all at once. Beat until almost incorporated. Stop the mixer and remove the bowl from the mixer. Add the walnuts and chocolate chips and incorporate the rest of the ingredients with a spatula.

Spoon mixture into loaf pan. Bake for 45 minutes to 1 hour, or until a skewer inserted in the center of the loaf comes out clean.

Remove from the oven and allow loaf to cool in the pan for 20 minutes before inverting onto a wire rack to cool completely. Serve with milky coffee and enjoy.

Banana bread will keep for up to 5 days, well wrapped, at room temperature.

giant mint chocolate chip marshmallow cubes

makes 16 giant marshmallow cubes

When I was a kid, I was absolutely smitten by dehydrated space ice cream. It was packaged freeze-dried ice cream sold at the science museum. Astronauts eat ice cream in space! Am I the only dork who remembers this stuff?

This is my kick-butt interpretation of those packaged dried ice cream pucks. This is where marshmallows meet ice cream. Consider this portable ice cream. You might want to stick one in your pocket and go to space—good luck with that! I hope Saturn is cool.

1 cup powdered sugar	2 cups granulated sugar	2 cups (12 ounces) semisweet
1 cup cold water	⅔ cup light corn syrup	chocolate chips
3 (¼-ounce) envelopes	¼ teaspoon salt	
unflavored gelatin	1 teaspoon mint extract	

Grease an 8-inch-square pan and shake powdered sugar through the pan, coating generously.

Pour ½ cup of the water into the bowl of an electric stand mixer fitted with a whisk attachment. Pour the gelatin over the cold water and let sit while you prepare the other ingredients.

In a medium saucepan over medium heat, add remaining ½ cup water, granulated sugar, corn syrup, and salt. Stir gently until sugar dissolves then attach a candy thermometer and heat mixture until it reaches 240 degrees F. Mixture does not need to be stirred once the sugar is dissolved.

Turn the mixer on low speed. Carefully drizzle the hot sugar mixture into the gelatin in a steady stream. Try to prevent the stream of hot sugar from hitting the whisk attachment. That will only spatter hot sugar across the sides of the bowl. Once sugar is incorporated, gradually increase speed to high and whip mixture until white and thick, about 12 minutes. Stop the mixture, add mint extract and beat for another 3 minutes.

Feel the bottom of the mixing bowl with your hand. The mixture should be slightly warm, but not hot: just warm to the touch. The sugar mixture will have cooled slightly during the mixing process. Add the chocolate chips once the mixture has cooled slightly, so as to not completely melt the chocolate.

Scrape marshmallow mixture into prepared pan. Smooth the top. If you're fighting with the sticky mixture, use a wet spatula to smooth everything over. Dust powdered sugar over the top of the marshmallow and let sit, uncovered, overnight or for at least 4 hours.

Lightly dust a cutting board with powdered sugar. Turn the marshmallow block out onto cutting board and slice into 16 large squares. Toss each marshmallow in powdered sugar to coat all sides. Enjoy in coffee or hot chocolate, or toasted for the biggest S'mores treat of your life.

Marshmallows keep, well wrapped, at room temperature for up to 2 weeks.

chocolate fudge brownies with chocolate buttercream frosting

makes one 8-inch pan

You might be surprised by the problems that a nice batch of brownies can solve. Late for a dentist appointment? Bring brownies. Fight with your best friend? Bring brownies. Want to find out if your cute neighbor is single or attached? Stop by with a batch of brownies and scope out the décor. There is no situation that doesn't call for these delightfully dense chocolate-covered brownies. See for yourself.

¾ cup all-purpose flour

1 teaspoon baking powder

½ teaspoon salt

½ cup (1 stick) unsalted butter

3 ounces unsweetened chocolate

½ cup packed brown sugar

½ cup granulated sugar

2 large eggs

1 large egg yolk

1 teaspoon pure vanilla extract

½ cup semisweet chocolate chips

Place a rack in the upper third of the oven and preheat to 350 degrees F. Grease and flour an 8-inch-square baking dish and set aside.

In a medium bowl, whisk together flour, baking powder, and salt. Set aside.

Bring about 2 inches of water to a boil in a medium saucepan. In a medium, heatproof bowl, add butter and unsweetened chocolate. Place the bowl over, but not touching, the simmering water and allow to melt. Stir to incorporate. Once melted, remove the bowl from the simmering pot. Whisk in brown and granulated sugars. Whisk in eggs, yolk, and vanilla. Add the flour mixture, all at once, to the chocolate mixture. Fold together with a spatula until well incorporated. Fold in chocolate chips.

Pour batter into prepared pan and bake for 25 to 30 minutes. Bake until a skewer inserted in the center of the brownie comes out clean. Remove from the oven and cool completely before frosting.

Frost with a half recipe of The Best Chocolate Buttercream Frosting (p. 133) when cooled.

Brownies last, well wrapped, at room temperature for up to 5 days.

crunchy cocoa roasted nuts

makes 3 cups nuts

Roasted almonds are a delight. Roasted almonds coated in a crunchy chocolate meringue are an extra-super delight. I love these nuts with just a touch of cayenne pepper to kick up the flavor. The spice keeps me coming back for handful after handful.

3 cups raw almonds

6 tablespoons (¾ stick)
   unsalted butter

2 large egg whites

1 teaspoon salt

1 cup granulated sugar

3 tablespoons unsweetened
   cocoa powder

⅛ teaspoon cayenne pepper

Place a rack in the center of the oven and preheat to 350 degrees F.

Place almonds on a baking sheet and roast for 15 minutes in the oven. Remove from oven and place in a medium bowl to cool completely.

Place butter on rimmed baking sheet and melt in the oven for 5 to 7 minutes. Remove from the oven and set aside.

In the bowl of an electric stand mixer fitted with a whisk attachment, add egg whites and ½ teaspoon of the salt. Beat on medium speed until frothy. Gradually add sugar. Increase the mixer to medium-high and beat until white and glossy and the egg whites hold almost stiff peaks.

Add the remaining ½ teaspoon salt, the cocoa powder, and cayenne pepper, and beat until well incorporated.

Pour the egg mixture over the toasted almonds and toss together until almonds are evenly coated. Spoon mixture atop the melted butter on the rimmed baking sheet. Bake for 30 to 40 minutes, removing the pan from the oven to toss almonds 2 or 3 times during baking.

Remove from the oven and allow to cool completely before serving. Almonds will keep, in an airtight container, at room temperature for up to a week.

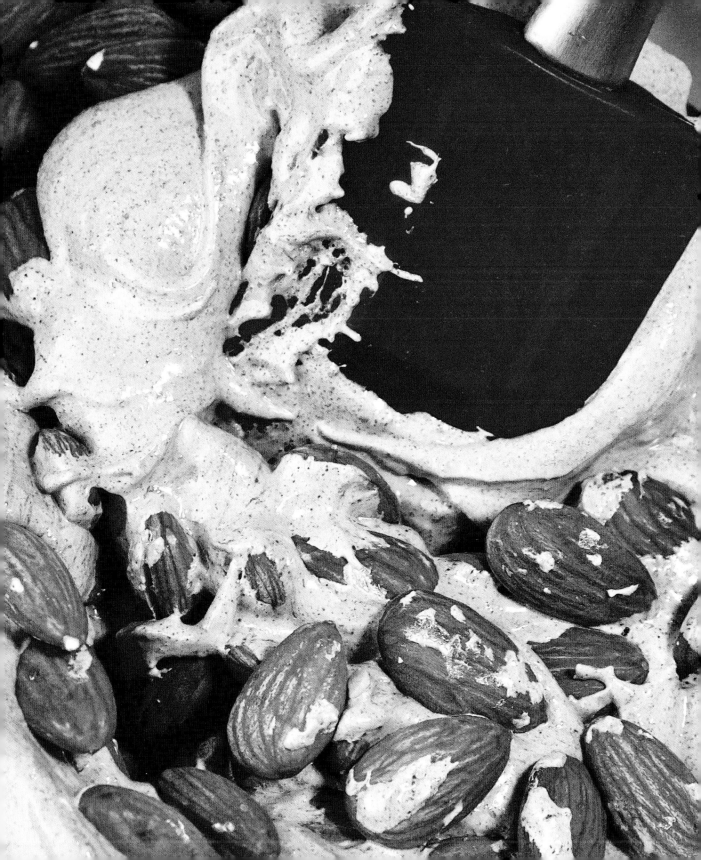

chocolate and salty peanut butter ice cream

makes 1 quart ice cream

Sit down. Take a deep breath. This is about to get real. This chocolate peanut butter ice cream is dangerously good. It doesn't hold back on utter richness and salty appeal. It's not breaking news that peanut butter and chocolate are a match made in heaven, so I feel like this ice cream might just be a classic—like pearls and heels. Edible, delicious, pearls and heels.

For the chocolate ice cream:

1 cup granulated sugar

⅓ cup unsweetened cocoa powder

¼ teaspoon salt

3 tablespoons cornstarch

2½ cups whole milk

¾ cup heavy cream

¾ cup semisweet chocolate chips

For the peanut butter filling:

½ cup smooth salted peanut butter
    (I like natural peanut butter)

1 tablespoon heavy cream

Pinch of salt

To make the chocolate ice cream: in a small bowl, whisk together sugar, cocoa powder, salt, and cornstarch.

In a medium saucepan, warm milk over medium heat. Add the sugar mixture and whisk any lumps out as the milk heats. Heat until the mixture just begins to boil and thickens to a warm pudding consistency. Cornstarch thickens at the boiling point, so once the mixture boils, it's just about done cooking. Remove from heat and pour through a fine-mesh strainer into a medium bowl. Stir in the cream and chocolate chips until melted and smooth. Place plastic wrap directly over the custard and refrigerate until completely cool.

While the mixture cools, make the peanut butter filling. Whisk together peanut butter, cream, and salt. Cover with plastic wrap and set aside at room temperature.

When custard mixture is completely cooled, churn it according to ice cream maker instructions. When completely churned, spoon into a freezer-friendly container. Drizzle in the peanut butter mixture and gently swirl with a butter knife. Don't overwork the peanut butter. Make sure there are large peanut butter swirls throughout. Store in the freezer for several hours before serving.

Ice cream will last, in an airtight container, in the freezer for up to a week.

chocolate raspberry fudge pops

makes 12 fudge pops

I need to always have milk in the fridge, fancy shampoo in the shower, and some sort of chocolate treat in the freezer. These fudge pops totally fit the bill. Essentially, they are frozen chocolate pudding with fresh raspberries and dark chocolate chunks—totally kid-friendly, but totally grown-up, too.

½ cup granulated sugar

2 tablespoons cornstarch

3 tablespoons unsweetened
   cocoa powder

Pinch of salt

2 cups whole milk

½ cup heavy cream

1 teaspoon pure vanilla extract

1 tablespoon unsalted butter

1 cup fresh raspberries,
   very coarsely chopped

½ cup dark chocolate chunks

In a small bowl, whisk together sugar, cornstarch, cocoa, and salt.

In a medium saucepan, heat milk over medium heat. Whisk the sugar mixture into the milk as it heats. Heat mixture until it thickens into a warm pudding. Cornstarch thickens at the boiling point, so once the mixture boils, it's pretty much done. When thick, remove from heat and add cream, vanilla, and butter. Stir until melted.

Place plastic wrap directly over the custard and store in the refrigerator until completely cooled.

Once cooled, fold in the raspberries and chocolate chunks. Divide mixture between ice pop molds, or small paper cups, top with sticks, and freeze until solid.

To remove the frozen pops, run the containers under warm water and tug gently at the sticks until loosened.

Fudge pops will last, stored in the freezer, for up to a week.

cocoa almond granola

makes 8 cups granola

We're moving into major midnight snack territory. This crunchy, almond-studded granola is absolutely perfect between the hours of 10 p.m. and 2 a.m. You'll swear it was sent down directly from heaven. This granola doesn't have an overwhelmingly cocoa flavor. It's subtle, but just rich enough to feel like a healthy, crunchy, and lightly decadent before-bedtime snack.

4 cups old-fashioned oats

1 cup raw whole almonds

1 cup sweetened shredded coconut

1½ teaspoons ground cinnamon

2 tablespoons unsweetened
    cocoa powder

½ teaspoon salt

½ cup granulated sugar

¼ cup honey

⅓ cup vegetable oil

2 tablespoons butter

2 teaspoons pure vanilla extract

Place a rack in the center and upper third of the oven and preheat to 350 degrees F. Line 1 large or 2 small baking sheets with parchment paper and set aside.

In a large bowl, toss together oats, almonds, coconut, cinnamon, cocoa powder, and salt. Set aside.

In a medium saucepan, combine sugar, honey, oil, and butter. Stir over medium heat until sugar dissolves and mixture begins to bubble. Remove from heat and stir in vanilla.

Pour the warm sugar mixture over the oat mixture and toss with a wooden spoon. Toss until all of the oat and almond bits are at least moistened by the sugar mixture. Spoon mixture onto prepared baking sheet(s) and place in the oven.

Bake granola for 30 minutes, removing from the oven to toss and stir 2 to 3 times during baking. Granola is done when it is toasted around the edges and fragrant.

Remove from the oven and let cool completely. Store in an airtight container, at room temperature, for up to 2 weeks.

chocolate peanut butter ball cookies

makes 12 to 16 cookies

Every Christmas, my mom makes a dessert she calls Peanut Butter Balls. They're balls of peanut butter, butter, and sugar dipped in chocolate. You might know these little dreams as Buckeyes. I've taken inspiration from Mom's recipe and placed these decadent peanut butter balls atop chewy and rich brownie cookies. I never was one for sticking to the rules, and these cookies are all the better for it.

For the peanut butter balls:
2½ cups powdered sugar
6 tablespoons (¾ stick)
    unsalted butter, softened
6 tablespoons peanut butter

Few pinches of salt
For the cookies:
¼ cup all-purpose flour
¼ teaspoon baking powder
Pinch of salt

⅔ cup granulated sugar
2 large eggs
2 tablespoons unsalted butter
1⅓ cups semisweet chocolate chips
½ teaspoon pure vanilla extract

To make the peanut butter balls: in a large bowl, combine powdered sugar, butter, peanut butter, and salt. With clean hands, begin to work the mixture together. The butter and peanut butter should come together to create a stiff but pliable dough. Roll dough between your palms to create 16 small walnut-sized balls. Place on a clean cutting board or cookie sheet, cover loosely with plastic wrap, and set aside.

Place a rack in the center and upper third of the oven and preheat to 350 degrees F. Line 2 baking sheets with parchment paper and set aside.

To make the cookies: in a small bowl, whisk together flour, baking powder, and salt. Set aside.

In a medium bowl, whisk together sugar and eggs until thick and pale. Set aside.

Place about 2 inches of water in a medium saucepan and bring to a simmer. In a heatproof bowl, combine butter and chips. Place the bowl over but not touching the simmering water. Heat until chocolate and butter have melted together. Remove bowl from the heat. Add the melted chocolate to the egg mixture and fold together. Once entirely incorporated, stir in the vanilla. Fold in the flour mixture with a spatula until thoroughly incorporated. The mixture will be glossy and loose.

Spoon heaping tablespoonfuls of cookie batter onto the baking sheet, spacing the batter 2 inches apart.

Bake for 10 minutes until crackled on top, but still fudgy in the center. Remove from oven and immediately press a peanut butter ball into the center of each cookie. The warmth will help meld the two together. Allow cookies to cool on the cookie sheet for 10 minutes before removing to a wire rack to cool completely.

Cookies will last, well wrapped, at room temperature for up to 4 days.

dark chocolate and anise biscotti

makes about 3 dozen biscotti

I used to think that I hated the flavor of black licorice—until I actually tasted it. I can only imagine all the black jelly beans I could have enjoyed, had I just taken a chance.

Soft biscotti without nuts are a dream—mostly because I don't have to worry about chipping my front teeth on a rock-hard almond with my morning coffee. When slightly underbaked, these cookies are soft and tender. When baked just right, they're crisp and enticing.

Because the anise seeds are slightly crushed in this recipe, the flavor is subtle, save for a few flavor explosions when you crunch down on an anise seed. Just lovely with chocolate…but then again, what isn't?

2 cups all-purpose flour

1½ teaspoons anise seeds, slightly crushed

1 teaspoon baking powder

¼ teaspoon salt

6 tablespoons (¾ stick) unsalted butter, softened

1 cup granulated sugar, plus more for sprinkling

2 large eggs

1 large egg yolk

¾ cup semisweet chocolate chunks

Place a rack in the center and upper third of the oven and preheat oven to 325 degrees F. Line 2 baking sheets with parchment paper and set aside.

In a medium bowl, whisk together flour, anise seeds, baking powder, and salt. Set aside.

In the bowl of an electric stand mixer fitted with a paddle attachment, cream butter and sugar on medium speed until light and fluffy, 3 to 5 minutes.

Reduce mixer speed to low, and add 1 of the eggs and egg yolk and beat until well incorporated, about 2 minutes.

Add the flour mixture, all at once, to the butter mixture and beat on low speed until well combined. Mixture may seem a bit dry, but that's okay. Add chocolate chunks and blend throughout.

Divide the dough between the prepared pans. If the dough is shaggy and crumbly, that's fine—just knead it together. Shape dough into logs about 1½ inches wide and 8 inches long. Beat the remaining egg, brush over the logs, and sprinkle generously with sugar.

Bake biscotti on both racks for 20 minutes. Swap racks and bake for another 15 to 20 minutes, until golden brown and baked through. Let biscotti rest until cool enough to handle. Use a serrated knife to gently slice biscotti into 1-inch-thick slices. Flip cut side up onto the baking sheet and bake for another 10 to 15 minutes. Biscotti will still be slightly soft to the touch, and that's just the way I like it. Let cool and enjoy with coffee.

Biscotti will last, in an airtight container, at room temperature for up to 2 weeks.

chocolate chocolate chocolate chip muffins

makes 12 muffins

I absolutely support any excuse to eat chocolate for breakfast, or chocolate for high tea, or chocolate for an afternoon snack. These triple-chocolate muffins are moist, with little pockets of dark chocolate and a drizzle of melted white chocolate. I like to eat these while sitting on the couch with my feet on the coffee table, drinking wine at 4:30 in the afternoon. But maybe that's just me. They're good anytime, but especially as an indulgent afternoon snack.

½ cup (1 stick) unsalted butter

5 ounces semisweet chocolate,
   coarsely chopped

2 cups all-purpose flour

1 teaspoon baking powder

1 teaspoon baking soda

½ teaspoon salt

1 teaspoon instant espresso powder,
   or 1 teaspoon vanilla extract

½ cup packed brown sugar

2 large eggs

⅔ cup buttermilk

1 cup (6 ounces) semisweet
   dark chocolate chunks

½ cup white chocolate chips

Place a rack in the upper third of the oven and preheat to 350 degrees F. Line a 12-cup muffin tin with paper liners and set aside.

Place about 2 inches of water in a small saucepan over medium heat and bring the water to a simmer. Place butter and coarsely chopped chocolate in a heatproof bowl and place over, but not touching, the simmering water to melt while stirring occasionally. Once melted, remove the bowl from the pot and set aside to cool slightly.

In a medium bowl, whisk together flour, baking powder, baking soda, salt, and espresso powder (if using).

Whisk the brown sugar into the slightly cooled chocolate mixture. Whisk the eggs, buttermilk, and vanilla (if using) into the mixture until well blended.

Add the flour mixture, all at once, to the chocolate mixture and fold with a spatula until no visible flour bits remain. Fold in the chocolate chunks.

Divide the batter between the prepared cups, and bake for 18 to 20 minutes, or until a skewer inserted in the center of the cake comes out clean. Remove from the oven and allow to cool in the pan for 5 minutes before removing to a wire rack to cool completely.

While muffins cool, place white chocolate in a heatproof bowl and melt over, but not touching, the same simmering water you used to melt the butter mixture. Once melted, liberally drizzle over the cooled muffins.

Muffins will last, well wrapped, at room temperature for up to 4 days.

chocolate and black pepper goat cheese truffles

makes about 20 truffles

Put your fancy pants on! These chocolate goat cheese truffles are way outside of the box. Chocolate is always delicious. Goat cheese is soft, bright, and tangy. Black peppercorns are earthy and spicy. The three of these things together are completely surprising and totally delicious. They're somewhere in between savory and sweet, and perfect for a not-so-sweet dessert option.

4 ounces dark chocolate,
    coarsely chopped
4 ounces fresh goat cheese,
    at room temperature

3 tablespoons granulated sugar
½ teaspoon pure vanilla extract
¼ teaspoon coarsely crushed
    black peppercorns

3 tablespoons unsweetened
    cocoa powder
Coarse sea salt

Place about 2 inches of water in a small saucepan, and place chocolate in a heatproof bowl. Set the bowl over, but not touching, the simmering water to melt the chocolate. Once chocolate is melted, remove bowl from the pot and set aside to cool slightly.

In a medium bowl, whisk together goat cheese, melted chocolate, sugar, vanilla, and peppercorns until fluffy and well incorporated. Cover the mixture in plastic wrap and refrigerate for 1 hour or until firm.

Once firm, portion a heaping teaspoon of the goat cheese mixture into clean hands and roll into a ball. Coat the bottom half of the ball in cocoa powder, place on a cookie sheet, and top with a few flakes of coarse sea salt. Serve slightly chilled.

Truffles will last, in an airtight container, in the refrigerator for up to 3 days.

single girl melty chocolate cake

makes 1 small cake (serves 1)

I feel as if I've hit the jackpot with this recipe. It's a single-serving, warm, dark chocolaty, lava cake. Cake for one! Cake just for you! Oh, man. This cake is as awesome as sleeping kittens, the first *Matrix* movie, and online shoe shopping. How can such an easy-to-prepare dessert also be so indulgent and delicious? It's heaven-sent.

1 tablespoon unsalted butter	1 large egg	Pinch of salt
¼ cup semisweet chocolate chips	4 teaspoons granulated sugar	1 teaspoon all-purpose flour

Place a rack in the center of the oven and preheat oven to 375 degrees F. Place a cookie sheet in the oven as the oven heats.

Generously butter and flour a ¾- or 1-cup ramekin. Set aside.

In a small pot, bring 2 inches of water to a simmer.

Place butter and chocolate in a heatproof bowl and place over, but not touching, the simmering water. Stir until chocolate has melted. Allow to cool slightly.

In a small bowl, whisk together egg and sugar. Pour in the melted chocolate mixture, and whisk together until well incorporated. Add the salt and flour and stir until just combined.

Pour batter into prepared ramekin and place in the oven atop the cookie sheet. Bake for 7 to 10 minutes. The less time in the oven, the more gooey the cake will be.

Remove from the oven. Allow to cool for 2 minutes. Using pot holders, carefully invert cake onto a plate and dig in. Cake will be gooey and melty and slightly underdone—super delicious!

This cake is intended for immediate consumption (duh).

dark chocolate ganache tart with fresh berries and sweetened cream

makes one 9-inch tart

I didn't own a fancy tart pan (the kind with the removable bottom) until last year. I thought they were for professional French bakers, or people whose kitchens were stocked to the nines. Turns out I was wrong. My tart pan has been such a fun addition to my totally understocked kitchen. My tart pan makes everything that comes out of it feel fancy and full of class. This chocolate dessert is no exception.

The tart is dark and creamy and undeniably rich. The baked crust is kicked up with a bit of cinnamon and ginger, a surprising complement to the chocolate and fresh berries. It's a class act.

For the tart crust:
1½ cups all-purpose flour
½ cup powdered sugar
½ teaspoon salt
½ teaspoon ground cinnamon
Scant ⅛ teaspoon ground ginger
½ cup (1 stick) unsalted butter, cold
1 large egg yolk, beaten

For the ganache:
8 ounces dark chocolate, finely chopped
1¼ cups heavy cream
¼ cup (½ stick) unsalted butter, at room temperature, cut in half

For the topping:
1 cup heavy cream
3 tablespoons powdered sugar
1 cup fresh raspberries
½ cup fresh blackberries, cut in half

To make the tart crust: in a large bowl, combine flour, sugar, salt, and spices. Cut in butter with fingers until well incorporated. Some butter chunks will be the size of small pebbles, others will resemble oatmeal flakes. Once incorporated, add the egg yolk and bring mixture together with a fork. The mixture will be shaggy and crumbly; not to worry. Dump the entire mixture into a tart pan with a removable bottom. Use your fingers to press the crust into the sides and on the bottom of the pan. Place tart crust in the freezer to chill for an hour. This step is important; it will keep the tart crust from puffing up too much during baking.

While the tart shell chills, make the ganache: add chocolate pieces to a medium bowl. In a small saucepan over medium heat, bring the cream to a very low simmer. Pour half of the heated cream on top of the chocolate pieces and allow to rest for 1 minute. The chocolate will begin melting. With a whisk, begin to incorporate melted chocolate into the cream. Start by whisking in the center, working your way out to carefully incorporate the cream and the melting chocolate. Slowly add the remaining cream and whisk carefully until smooth and glossy. Add the butter chunks and use a spatula to stir until the butter is melted. The mixture should be dark and glossy. Set aside, at room temperature while the tart crust bakes.

Place a rack in the upper third of the oven and preheat to 350 degrees F. Butter a piece of foil and place, butter side down, on top of the chilled tart shell. Bake for 20 minutes. Remove buttered foil and bake for another 15 minutes, or until the tart shell is golden brown. Allow to cool completely before filling with ganache.

To make the topping: in a medium bowl, whisk together cream and sugar until soft peaks form. Spread the chocolate ganache inside of the cooled tart shell. Top with fresh berries. In the center, generously dollop whipped cream. Serve immediately.

I like this tart the day it is made, but tart will last, well wrapped and refrigerated, for up to 3 days.

chocolate hazelnut spread with orange cream cheese grilled sandwiches

makes 1 sandwich

I am an adult, and I will do what I want. I might jaywalk, I double-park, or park in a red zone. I might get a doozy of a ticket for all of those things, but this sandwich—oh man—is totally within bounds. Rich chocolate hazelnut spread is combined with orangey cream cheese melted together between two slices of eggy challah bread. Decadent adulthood—I love it.

½ tablespoon butter

2 tablespoons cream cheese, softened

½ teaspoon orange zest

Pinch of salt

2 slices challah or sourdough bread

2 tablespoons chocolate hazelnut spread

Set a frying pan over medium-low heat and place the butter in the pan to melt.

In a small bowl, mix together cream cheese, orange zest, and salt. Mix until cream cheese is soft, spreadable, and very well incorporated.

Spread cream cheese mixture on one side of 1 piece of bread. Spread chocolate hazelnut spread on the other slice of bread. Sandwich the two spread sides together and place in the heated pan. Grill on either side until golden brown and melty.

Let sandwich rest for 2 minutes before slicing in half and enjoying. This sandwich is best eaten immediately.

chocolate malt bread pudding

makes one 8-inch dish

I don't like bread pudding. Ick! I have two very concrete exceptions to this rule. I like bread pudding with chocolate, and I like bread pudding with booze. Really though, most things are made better with chocolate and booze.

This bread pudding is a pretty stellar combination of chocolate, cream, and sugar. Malt powder is a fun twist that's not immediately recognizable, but is immediately tasty. Served with a scoop of vanilla ice cream, and hot fudge sauce (p. 83), this bread pudding comes alive.

5 loosely packed cups stale
    challah bread (about 8 slices
    ripped into large chunks)
1½ cups whole milk
¾ cup heavy cream

2 large eggs
2 large egg yolks
⅓ cup granulated sugar
Pinch of salt

½ cup semisweet chocolate chunks,
    finely chopped
¼ cup plus 2 tablespoons malt powder
1 teaspoon pure vanilla extract

Place a rack in the center of the oven and preheat to 350 degrees F. Lightly butter an 8-inch-square baking dish. Set aside.

If your bread isn't stale, place the bread chunks on a baking sheet and toast for 10 minutes in oven. Place stale bread in buttered baking dish.

In a small saucepan, heat together the milk and cream. Heat until just barely boiling.

In a medium bowl, whisk together eggs, egg yolks, sugar, and salt. While whisking, slowly drizzle warmed milk mixture into the egg mixture to temper the eggs. Slowly add all the milk. Once well incorporated, add the chocolate chunks, malt powder, and vanilla, and whisk until the chocolate is melted.

Pour the creamy chocolate mixture over the bread chunks. Make sure the majority of bread is submerged and let rest for 30 minutes.

Place the bread pudding in the oven and bake for 25 to 35 minutes or until the top looks dry and dull and the pudding is set, not milky and jiggly.

Carefully remove from the oven and allow to rest for 20 minutes before serving warm. Bread pudding is also delicious at room temperature. Top with vanilla ice cream and hot fudge for a decadent treat.

Bread pudding will last, well wrapped, in the refrigerator for up to 3 days, although I like it best the day it is baked.

chocolate bundt cake with chocolate sour cream glaze

makes one 10-inch Bundt cake

This cake is a major crowd pleaser and no one has to know just how easy it is. There is no need for a stand mixer, just a few bowls and a spatula.

Coffee, cocoa, and sour cream are the magic ingredients in the cake. The result is a super moist chocolate cake that tastes exactly what a cake mix cake would taste like if it didn't taste so much like … cake mix.

The glaze is a snap. The chocolate intensity can range from dark to milk, depending on how sweet you like your frosting.

For the cake:

1¼ cups hot prepared coffee

1 cup unsweetened cocoa powder

2½ cups all-purpose flour

1¼ teaspoons salt

2½ teaspoons baking soda

2 cups granulated sugar

3 large eggs

1¼ cups sour cream

1 cup plus 2 tablespoons vegetable oil

For the glaze:

¾ cup (1½ sticks) butter

1 cup (6 ounces) semisweet chocolate

4 tablespoons hot prepared coffee

⅓ cup sour cream,
    at room temperature

Place a rack in the center of the oven and preheat to 350 degrees F. Grease and flour a 10-inch Bundt pan and set aside.

To make the cake: in a small bowl, whisk together coffee and cocoa powder until smooth and no lumps remain. Set aside.

In a large bowl, whisk together flour, salt, and baking soda. Set aside.

In a medium bowl, whisk together sugar and eggs until thick and pale. Add the sour cream and oil, and carefully whisk until well incorporated. Add the egg mixture, all at once, to the flour mixture. Whisk carefully to incorporate. Once no flour bits remain, add the coffee mixture, and gently whisk to incorporate. The batter will be loose and smooth.

Pour batter into prepared pan and bake for 45 to 60 minutes, or until a skewer inserted in the cake comes out clean.

Remove from oven and allow to cool in the pan for 20 minutes before inverting onto a wire rack to cool completely. Cake should be completely cool before frosting.

To make the glaze: place 2 inches of water in a medium pan and bring to a simmer. Place butter and chocolate in a heat-proof bowl. Place the bowl over, but not touching, the simmering water. Stir until chocolate has melted.

Remove from the heat and let cool just a bit. Stir in 2 tablespoons of the hot coffee, followed by the sour cream. Add the remaining 2 tablespoons coffee and stir until glossy.

Use a butter knife to spread glaze onto cooled cake. Cake will last, well wrapped, in the refrigerator for up to 4 days.

easy white chocolate mousse

makes 4 to 6 servings

When melted white chocolate meets whipped cream, I swear, you can call it chocolate mousse, or at least cheaters chocolate mousse. But totally chocolate mousse, all the same.

2 tablespoons water

2 tablespoons unsalted butter

6 ounces white chocolate chunks

1¼ cups heavy cream

2 teaspoons powdered sugar

Pinch of salt

1 large egg yolk, beaten

In a medium saucepan over medium-low heat, combine water, butter, and chocolate. Stir until chocolate is melted. Remove from heat and place mixture in a medium bowl to cool slightly.

In the bowl of an electric stand mixer fitted with a whisk attachment, combine cream, sugar, and salt. Begin with mixer on medium speed, gradually increasing to medium high, beat until stiff peaks form. Remove the bowl from the mixer and set aside.

By now, the chocolate should be just warmer than body temperature. Whisk in the egg yolk until combined.

Add half of the chocolate mixture to the whipped cream. Fold together until just incorporated. Add the remaining chocolate mixture and fold together until just incorporated. Try not to overmix the mixture and deflate the whipped cream. Transfer mousse to smaller bowl. Place a piece of plastic wrap directly over the mousse, and refrigerate for at least 2 hours before scooping and serving.

Mousse will last, in an airtight container, at room temperature for up to 3 days.

chocolate covered coconut macaroon ice cream

makes 1 quart

This coconut ice cream is amazingly delicious, and couldn't possibly get any more coconutty. I've loaded it with toasted coconut, so every bite has a mouthful. But the absolute star of this dessert is the chocolate topping. Friends, seriously! I made a homemade Magic Shell. Take a moment—I didn't even know this was possible.

Coconut oil and melted dark chocolate combine, and when drizzled over cold ice cream, harden to a crispy shell. It's delicious, all natural, and so so fun to eat. This dessert is coconut from head to toe.

For the ice cream:
1 (14-ounce) can coconut milk
1 (14-ounce) can light coconut milk
Scant 1 cup granulated sugar

1½ cups unsweetened shredded coconut
For the chocolate shell:
¾ cup coarsely chopped semisweet chocolate

½ cup coconut oil
Pinch of salt

In a medium saucepan, combine coconut milks and sugar. Stir over medium heat until sugar dissolves. Place milk mixture in a medium bowl, cover with plastic wrap, and place in the refrigerator to cool completely.

Place a rack in the upper third of the oven and preheat to 350 degrees F. Place shredded coconut on an ungreased baking sheet and bake for 6 to 8 minutes, until browned and fragrant. Keep an eye on the coconut; remove from the oven and stir as necessary to ensure even browning. Coconut cooks quickly! Remove from oven and place in a small bowl to cool completely.

Once the milk mixture has cooled, churn in an ice cream maker according to manufacturer's instructions. Once the mixture is almost entirely churned, add the roasted coconut and churn until well mixed and the consistency of soft-serve frozen yogurt.

Place in a freezer-safe container and put in the freezer to harden.

While the ice cream hardens, make the chocolate shell. Place 2 inches of water in a medium saucepan and bring to a simmer. Place chocolate, coconut oil, and salt in a heat-proof bowl and place over, but not touching, simmering water. Stir until chocolate melts and mixture is well blended. Remove bowl from simmering water and place in a squeeze bottle or jar. Chocolate shell should be kept at room temperature. Coconut oil turns to a liquid when kept above 75 degrees. If the chocolate shell hardens, it can be reheated in the microwave for a few seconds.

To serve, scoop ice cream into a bowl and top with chocolate shell. Chocolate will harden when it touches the cold ice cream.

Ice cream will last, in a freezer-safe container, for up to 7 days. Chocolate shell will last, at room temperature, for up to 2 weeks.

sweet potato chocolate chip cookies

makes about 2 dozen cookies

I support any opportunity to turn sweet potatoes into dessert. Their bright orange flesh lends itself so beautifully to sweet treats. These soft, cakey cookies are proof positive. Add chocolate…just because!

1 medium sweet potato

2 cups all-purpose flour
   (or half whole wheat flour)

1½ teaspoons baking powder

1 teaspoon baking soda

1 teaspoon ground cinnamon

¼ teaspoon ground cloves

¼ teaspoon ground coriander

2 large eggs

1 cup packed brown sugar

½ cup vegetable oil

2 teaspoons pure vanilla extract

1 cup (6 ounces) semisweet
   chocolate chips

Place a rack in the upper third of the oven and preheat to 400 degrees F.

Clean and scrub potato. Pierce the flesh with a fork, and place on a baking sheet lined with parchment paper. Bake until a knife inserted into the thickest part of the potato meets no resistance (about 40 minutes). Remove from the oven and allow to sit until cool enough to handle. Once cool, peel the skin away, thoroughly mash the flesh, to yield 1 cup.

Reduce oven temperature to 350 degrees F. Line a baking sheet with parchment paper. Set aside.

In a large bowl, whisk together flour, baking powder, baking soda, and spices. Set aside.

In a medium bowl, whisk together eggs and brown sugar until thick and pale. Carefully whisk in the oil and vanilla. Fold in the mashed sweet potato.

Add the egg mixture, all at once, to the flour mixture. Fold together with a spatula until no flour bits remain. Fold in the chocolate chips.

Scoop cookie dough, by the heaping tablespoonful, onto prepared baking sheet 2 inches apart. Bake for 10 to 12 minutes, until puffed and a skewer inserted into the center of one of the cookies comes out clean. Remove from the oven and allow to cool on the sheet for 10 minutes before removing to a wire rack to cool completely.

Cookies will last, well wrapped, at room temperature for up to 4 days. If storing the cookies in layers, separate the layers with parchment or waxed paper so they don't stick together.

6

have dessert, will travel

the best desserts to take to a party, ship to a friend, or sell at a bake sale.

The best part about making a beautiful cake is a) getting to lick the uncooked batter off the spatula, b) filling the kitchen with the smell of baked sugar and butter, and c) sharing that creation with friends—in that order.

But how do you get cakes and cookies from the oven to the dessert table at your friend's house across town? First, hold your breath. Second, pack up the cake and say a prayer. Third, avoid potholes.

Here are some recipes that are easy to pack up and take on the go, because sugar is best when it's shared.

cream cheese pound cake

makes one 9x5-inch loaf

If I could add glitter and sparkles to the name of this pound cake, I totally would. The name of this cake sells it short. This pound cake is deceptively simple, but a powerhouse dessert. Cream cheese works overtime to moisten this cake. Even when it's a little overbaked (let's face it—we all occasionally forget to set the timer), this cake is tender and moist. This pound cake rises like a champion and has a very browned, crackled, and crusty top. The inside, though, is just a flavorful and tender delight.

Top this cake with fresh berries or sliced peaches and barely sweetened whipped cream, enjoy it plain with black coffee, or toast it and top it with jam for afternoon tea. Any way you slice it, this cake is a beauty queen.

2 cups all-purpose flour

1½ teaspoons baking powder

½ teaspoon salt

1 (8-ounce) package cream cheese, softened

¾ cup (1½ sticks) unsalted butter, softened

1½ cups granulated sugar

2 teaspoons pure vanilla extract

4 large eggs

Place a rack in the center of the oven and preheat to 325 degrees F. Grease and flour a 9x5-inch loaf pan. Set aside.

In a medium bowl, whisk together flour, baking powder, and salt. Set aside.

In the bowl of an electric stand mixer fitted with a paddle attachment, beat cream cheese until soft and pliable. Add butter and sugar and beat until fluffy, about 3 minutes. Add the vanilla and stir until blended. Add eggs 1 at a time, beating on medium for 1 minute after each addition. Stop the mixer and scrape down the sides of the bowl as necessary.

With the mixer on low, add the flour mixture and beat until just incorporated. Stop the mixer and finish folding together the batter with a spatula.

Spoon batter into prepared pan and bake for 30 minutes. After 30 minutes, check on the cake, rotate it, and move to an upper rack if it's browning too quickly.

Bake for another 30 to 35 minutes, until a skewer inserted in the center of the cake comes out clean. Let cake cool in pan for 20 minutes before inverting onto a wire rack to cool completely.

Cake will last, well wrapped, at room temperature for up to 4 days.

lemon-lime and thyme cookies

makes about 4 dozen cookies

I have a problem leaving well enough alone. I can't make a plain batch of sugar cookies without scouring my kitchen to find something kooky to add to the dough. In this case, citrus and herbs make a subtle but unique addition to traditional sugar cookies. Lemon and lime are entirely familiar in sweet recipes. Thyme, though not traditional in this setting, knows how to pull its act together to meld with the citrus, butter, and sugar. The result is a flavorful and aromatic sweet biscuit.

3 cups all-purpose flour
¾ teaspoon baking powder
¼ teaspoon salt
2 teaspoons lemon zest
1 teaspoon lime zest

1 cup granulated sugar,
   plus more for sprinking
1 cup (2 sticks) unsalted butter,
   softened
2 teaspoons chopped fresh thyme

2 large eggs
1 tablespoon milk

In a medium bowl, whisk together flour, baking powder, and salt. Set aside.

On a clean board or counter, use a bench knife or the back of a spoon to rub the citrus zest into the sugar. The zest will become slightly yellow in color and fragrant.

In the bowl of an electric stand mixer fit with a paddle attachment, cream butter with citrus sugar on medium speed until pale and fluffy. Add thyme and blend well. Add 1 of the eggs and the milk, and beat for 1 minute.

Stop the mixer and scrape down the sides of the bowl. Add the flour mixture and beat on low speed until just combined. Remove the bowl from the mixer and finish incorporating ingredients with a spatula.

Place dough on a large piece of waxed paper and shape into a log. Roll cookie batter inside the waxed paper, crimp and seal the ends of the waxed paper, and refrigerate until chilled through, at least 3 hours, although overnight is best. This dough can be refrigerated for up to 4 days or frozen for up to a month.

When ready to roll out the cookies, remove the dough from the fridge and allow to soften for about 20 minutes.

Place a rack in the center and upper third of the oven, and preheat oven to 325 degrees F. Line 2 baking sheets with parchment paper and set aside.

Divide the dough in half and, on a lightly floured surface with a lightly floured rolling pin, roll one piece out to a ⅛-inch thickness. Use a round or festive-shaped cookie cutter to cut out cookies and place on prepared baking sheet. Before baking, mix remaining 1 egg with 1 tablespoon water. Brush cookies with the egg wash and sprinkle generously with sugar. Bake for 8 to 10 minutes, until just barely browned around the edges.

Allow cookies to rest on the baking sheet for 5 minutes before removing to a wire rack to cool completely.

Press the dough back together once to roll out again, then discard the dough as it will be a little overworked.

Cookies will last, well wrapped, at room temperature for up to 4 days.

avocado pound cake

makes two 9x5-inch loaves

My dad is the only person allowed to handle avocados in my family. Avocados are a very precious commodity, and in the hands of my father, reach their true potential: fresh homemade guacamole.

Leave it to me to completely diverge from family rules. I developed this recipe out of my obsession with sweet avocado recipes. After a failed avocado milkshake and a disastrous avocado pancake, this pound cake totally satisfied my obsession. It's sweet, green, and has a slight bite from cornmeal. Yes, this cake is green, and tastes like avocado, but it's surprisingly delicious. Try it! You'll be pleasantly surprised.

3 cups all-purpose flour
½ cup yellow cornmeal
½ teaspoon salt
1½ teaspoons baking powder
1½ teaspoons baking soda

¾ cup (1½ sticks) unsalted butter, softened
3 cups granulated sugar
1 cup plus 2 tablespoons ripe mashed avocados

4 large eggs
2 teaspoons pure vanilla extract
¾ cup buttermilk

Place a rack in the center and upper third of the oven and preheat to 350 degrees F. Grease and flour two 9x5-inch loaf pans and set aside.

In a medium bowl, whisk together flour, cornmeal, salt, baking powder, and baking soda. Set aside.

In the bowl of an electric stand mixer fitted with a paddle attachment, beat butter and sugar on medium speed until light and fluffy, 3 to 5 minutes. Add avocado and beat for another 2 minutes. Stop mixer and scrape down the sides of the bowl as necessary.

Add eggs, one at a time, beating on medium speed for 1 minute after each addition. Stop the mixer and scrape down to make sure everything is thoroughly mixed. Beat in vanilla.

With the mixer on low speed, add half of the flour mixture. Beat until just incorporated. Add the buttermilk and the remaining flour mixture. Beat until just incorporated. Remove bowl from the stand mixer, and finish incorporating the batter with a spatula.

Divide the batter between the pans and bake on alternating racks for 30 minutes. After 30 minutes, rotate racks and bake for another 15 to 25 minutes, or until a skewer inserted in the center comes out clean. Let cool in pans for 20 minutes before inverting onto a wire rack to cool completely.

Cake will last, well wrapped, at room temperature for up to 4 days.

cranberry orange poppy seed cookies

makes about 3 dozen cookies

My favorite part of making slice-and-bake sugar cookies is slicing the dough. When loaded with things like dried cranberries, orange zest, and poppy seeds, each slice reveals a different mosaic of deliciousness. It's mesmerizing. I could slice for days, mostly because I'm a crazy person. Get cookie slicing. You might be a crazy person, too. This is my favorite slice-and-bake cookie from Dorie Greenspan and Deb from Smitten Kitchen.

2 cups all-purpose flour
Pinch of salt
1 cup (2 sticks) unsalted butter, softened

⅔ cup powdered sugar
1 large egg
1 large egg yolk
1 teaspoon pure vanilla extract

2 teaspoons orange zest
¾ cup dried cranberries
1 tablespoon poppy seeds

In a medium bowl, whisk together flour and salt. Set aside.

In the bowl of an electric stand mixer fitted with a paddle attachment, beat together the butter and sugar on medium speed until soft and creamy, about 2 minutes. Add egg, yolk, and vanilla, and beat until well blended, another 2 minutes. Stop the mixer to scrape down the bowl as necessary.

Add the flour mixture, orange zest, cranberries, and poppy seeds, all at once, to the egg mixture and beat on low speed until just incorporated. Stop the mixer and remove the bowl and finish incorporating the ingredients with a spatula.

Divide the dough in half and place each half on a sheet of waxed paper. Press each half into a log 1 inch in diameter. Roll into plastic wrap and store in the fridge to chill for at least 3 hours, although overnight is best.

When ready to bake, place racks in the middle and upper third of the oven and preheat to 350 degrees F. Line 2 baking sheets with parchment paper and set aside.

Remove the dough from the refrigerator, unwrap, and use a knife to slice dough into ⅓-inch-thick rounds. Place on baking sheet about 1 inch apart.

Bake for 12 to 15 minutes, or until barely browned around the edges. Remove from the oven and cool on the baking sheet for 10 minutes before removing to a wire rack to cool completely.

Cookies will last, well wrapped, at room temperature for up to 4 days.

trail mix cookies

makes about 3 dozen cookies

Say you and I and two cute gentlemen are out on an afternoon hike. Yeah, we totally go on afternoon hikes—just go with it! Do not—DO NOT—put me in charge of the bag of trail mix. First, I'm a notorious snacker. Second, I'm also a picker. This means that when you're ready for a healthy trail mix break, all you will find are a few peanuts and raisins left in the bag. I will have eaten all of the chocolate and dried fruit. I will be very sorry for this.

To alleviate any awkward apologies and save our friendship, I baked trail mix into oatmeal cookies. That way I can't pick out all the good stuff—I just have to eat all of the cookies. You've been warned.

2½ cups old-fashioned oats

1 cup all-purpose flour

1 cup whole wheat flour

1 teaspoon baking powder

1 teaspoon baking soda

¾ teaspoon salt

1 teaspoon ground cinnamon

1 cup (2 sticks) unsalted butter, softened

1 cup granulated sugar

1 cup packed brown sugar

2 large eggs

2 teaspoons vanilla extract

1 cup (6 ounces) peanut butter chips

1 cup M&M chocolate candy

1 cup coarsely chopped roasted and salted peanuts

½ cup golden raisins

Place a rack in the center and upper third of the oven and preheat to 350 degrees F. Line 2 baking sheets with parchment paper. Set aside.

In a medium bowl, whisk together oats, flours, baking powder, baking soda, salt, and cinnamon. Set aside.

In the bowl of an electric stand mixer fitted with a paddle attachment, beat together butter and sugars until light and fluffy, 3 to 5 minutes. Add eggs one at a time, beating on medium speed for 1 minute between each addition. Stop the mixer and scrape down the bowl as necessary. Beat in the vanilla until thoroughly incorporated.

Stop the mixer and add the flour mixture all at once. Beat on low speed until just incorporated. Add the peanut butter chips, M&M's, peanuts, and raisins. Remove the bowl from the mixer, and finish incorporating the cookie batter with a spatula.

Roll generous tablespoonfuls into balls and place on prepared baking sheet. Bake for 10 to 13 minutes or until lightly browned around the edges. Remove from oven and allow to cool on the cookie sheet for 10 minutes before removing to a wire rack to cool.

Enjoy with milk, or milky coffee, and a smile.

Cookies will last, in an airtight container, at room temperature for up to 5 days.

everything caramel corn

makes about 12 cups

Here's what happened. Let me explain. I took most everything out of my cupboard and poured caramel over it. It was sweet and salty, and such a good idea. My only advice: steer clear of the canned anchovies, Spam, and green olives. These items are not necessarily caramel-friendly.

For the popcorn mixture:

2 tablespoons vegetable oil

¼ cup yellow popcorn kernels

½ teaspoon salt

1 cup dry-roasted almonds

1½ cups pretzel sticks (2 big handfuls)

1½ cups cheese crackers or mini
  peanut butter sandwich crackers

For the caramel:

1 cup (2 sticks) unsalted butter

2 cups packed brown sugar

¾ cup light corn syrup

1 teaspoon salt

1 teaspoon baking soda

To make the popcorn mixture: in a large pan over medium-high heat, warm oil. Add the corn kernels and place a lid, slightly ajar, over the pot. Pop the popcorn until the popping sound subsides. Turn off the heat, carefully pour the hot popcorn into a large bowl and sprinkle with the salt.

In a 9x13-inch pan, measure 7 heaping cups of popcorn, being sure to avoid any unpopped kernels. Top popcorn with almonds, pretzel sticks, and crackers. Set aside.

Place a rack in the center of the oven and preheat to 200 degrees F.

To make the caramel: combine butter, brown sugar, corn syrup, and salt in a medium, heavy-bottomed saucepan. Carefully whisk the mixture as it heats and the sugar melts. Boil the sugar and butter mixture for 5 minutes. Remove from heat and add baking soda. Whisk well. Carefully pour the sugar mixture into the 9x13-inch pan over the popcorn mixture. Use a large wooden spoon to toss the two together making sure that every bit of the popcorn mixture is coated in caramel. Be careful—you don't want the hot sugar to touch your hands. It burns!

Place pan in the oven and bake for 45 minutes, removing the pan to toss every 15 minutes. Once baked, remove from oven. Carefully spoon onto sheets of waxed paper to dry. Once dry, store in an airtight container.

Popcorn will last, stored in an airtight container, at room temperature for up to 1 week.

orange gingerbread squares with cream cheese frosting

makes one 8-inch pan

You know what gets me excited about the holidays? Mistletoe, holiday parties, those delicious-smelling clove oranges, giant Christmas trees, and chocolate-covered everything. I definitely was not excited about holiday gingerbread until this recipe fell into my life.

Gingerbread—I used to think, if you've had one, you've had them all. But listen up! I've injected this cake with orange zest and topped it with rich cream cheese frosting. Pomegranates on top make this cake shine like a jewel. And just like that, I'm all caught up in the holiday spirit.

2¼ cups all-purpose flour

2 teaspoons ground ginger

1 teaspoon ground cinnamon

¼ teaspoon ground cloves

1¾ teaspoons baking soda

½ teaspoon salt

¾ cup plus 2 tablespoons vegetable oil

¾ cup granulated sugar

2 large eggs

¾ cup unsulfured molasses
  (not blackstrap)

¼ cup honey

2 teaspoons orange zest

¾ cup hot water

1 recipe Cream Cheese Frosting
  (p. 136)

Pomegranate seeds for garnish

Place a rack in the center of the oven and preheat to 350 degrees F. Grease and flour an 8-inch-square baking pan. Set aside.

In a large bowl, whisk together flour, ginger, cinnamon, cloves, baking soda, and salt. Set aside.

In a medium bowl, whisk together vegetable oil, sugar, and eggs until thick and pale. Add molasses, honey, and orange zest, and whisk until well incorporated.

Add the egg mixture to the flour mixture and fold together with a spatula. Add the hot water, and carefully fold together until batter is smooth and velvety.

Pour batter into prepared dish and bake for 35 to 40 minutes or until a skewer inserted into the center of the cake comes out clean.

Remove from the oven and allow to cool completely in the pan before frosting.

Frost cake with Cream Cheese Frosting, top with pomegranate seeds, and cut into squares.

banana bourbon bread pudding

makes one 8-inch pan

Do not use this recipe as an excuse to buy a delicious, inviting, and tempting bottle of bourbon. As you're whipping up this bread pudding to bring to your neighbor's brunch, you're liable to put a splash of bourbon in your coffee and another splash in the bread pudding, and perhaps another dash or two in your coffee…again. Or wait, maybe that's just me. I'm a terrible example: be forewarned.

I love this bread pudding. Baked bananas and fresh bananas, soft bread and crisp bread tops, creamy custard and delicious bourbon. I love to serve this at brunches—it's entirely delicious.

1 stale baguette (about 10 ounces)

2 mashed bananas (about ⅔ cup)

2½ cups whole milk

¾ cup packed brown sugar

⅛ teaspoon salt

5 large eggs

3 tablespoons bourbon

2 teaspoons pure vanilla extract

Cinnamon sugar

2 sliced bananas for topping

Place a rack in the center of the oven and preheat to 350 degrees F. Butter an 8-inch-square baking dish. Set aside.

Tear stale baguette into small and large chunks. Place in the prepared baking dish. Add mashed bananas. With your hands, incorporate the mashed bananas among the torn bread. Mash together until bananas are evenly distributed among the bread chunks.

In a medium saucepan over low heat, combine milk, sugar, and salt. Stir until sugar is dissolved and milk is warm. Remove from heat and let cool slightly.

In a medium bowl, whisk eggs. While whisking, drizzle in the warm milk mixture. Whisk until all the milk is added and mixture is well incorporated. Stir in bourbon and vanilla.

Pour the milk mixture over the torn bread. Press the bread into the liquid so that all of the bread is at least moistened. Allow the mixture to rest for 10 minutes before baking.

Bake for 25 to 35 minutes, or until bread is browned and liquid is no longer jiggly, but the bread still appears somewhat moist. Remove from the oven and allow to cool for 20 minutes before serving. Top with cinnamon sugar and fresh sliced bananas.

I love this bread pudding warm, the day it is baked. Bread pudding will last, well wrapped, in the refrigerator for up to 3 days.

peach cobbler muffins

makes 12 muffins

Every summer I try to drown myself in peaches. Their soft, juicy flesh is just the stuff that my dreams are made of. Peach muffins are a simple and easy way to enjoy summer's fancy fruit. Fresh peach chunks are enrobed in a browned butter batter, and topped with a brown sugar and cinnamon streusel. It's a gorgeous summer muffin that is really wonderful with cinnamony black coffee.

For the muffins:

1½ cups all-purpose flour

½ cup granulated sugar

¼ cup packed brown sugar

1½ teaspoons baking powder

¾ teaspoon salt

½ teaspoon ground cinnamon

¼ teaspoon ground nutmeg

7 tablespoons (almost 1 stick) unsalted butter

1 large egg

1 large egg yolk

⅓ cup milk

2 teaspoons pure vanilla extract

1¼ cups diced peaches

For the topping:

3 tablespoons unsalted butter, cold

½ cup all-purpose flour

¼ cup packed brown sugar

Pinch of salt

Pinch of ground nutmeg

¼ teaspoon ground cinnamon

Place a rack in the upper third of the oven and preheat to 350 degrees F. Butter and flour a 12-cup muffin pan and set aside. You can also use cupcake papers for this recipe.

To make the muffins: in a medium bowl, whisk together flour, sugars, baking powder, salt, cinnamon, and nutmeg.

Place butter in a small saucepan, and melt until browned over medium heat. Remove from the heat and cool slightly.

In a medium bowl, whisk together egg, yolk, milk, and vanilla. While whisking, slowly drizzle in the warm butter, making sure to scrape any brown bits into the egg mixture as well. Whisk until well incorporated.

Add the milk mixture to the flour mixture all at once. Fold together with a spatula. Once no flour bits remain, fold in the diced peaches. Divide the batter between the muffin cups.

To make the topping: combine all the ingredients in a small bowl and blend together with your fingers until crumbly. Butter will be the size of oats and small pebbles. Divide the topping among the muffin cups on top of the batter.

Bake muffins for 15 to 18 minutes, or until a skewer inserted into the center of one of the muffins comes out clean. Remove from the oven and cool in the pan 20 minutes before removing. To remove, run a butter knife along the edges of the muffin pan and gently scoop out.

Muffins will last, well wrapped, at room temperature for up to 3 days.

pecan pralines

makes 12 to 16 pralines

I used to think that Pecan Pralines only existed in a magical place called New Orleans. As it turns out, Pecan Pralines are just about the easiest thing to make. Cook sugar with butter, add nuts, and spoon onto parchment paper. It doesn't get any easier. These candies are for those with a die-hard sweet tooth as they're profoundly sweet and rich.

1 cup packed brown sugar

1 cup granulated sugar

¼ teaspoon salt

½ cup heavy cream

2 cups pecan halves

3 tablespoons unsalted butter

Line 2 baking sheets with parchment paper or foil. Set aside.

Place a medium, heavy-bottomed saucepan over medium heat. Add brown sugar, granulated sugar, salt, and cream. Heat to boiling, turn the heat to low and continue cooking until all the sugar is dissolved and the mixture is smooth and bubbling.

Add pecans and butter to the mixture and cook, stirring, until butter is melted. Let mixture cook in a rolling simmer for 5 minutes.

Remove from heat and allow mixture to cool in the pan for 12 to 15 minutes. This will help the mixture solidify a bit, before being spooned into pralines.

Once mixture has cooled, use a tablespoon to generously spoon out praline portions onto the prepared pans. The pralines will be chunky and pecans will be piled on top of one another. Let pralines cool and harden at room temperature for at least 30 minutes before removing from the pan.

Pralines will keep, in an airtight container in layers separated by waxed paper, for up to a week.

flaxseed and cracked pepper crackers

makes about 4 dozen crackers

Crackers are one of the easiest things to pop into the kitchen and make. They're simple and impressive. People will do a double-take when they hear that you've shown up at their party and brought home-made crackers. Served with goat cheese, an aged cheddar cheese, or spicy hummus, these crackers shine. Oh! P.S. They're healthy, too.

¼ cup golden flaxseed

¼ cup ground flaxseed meal

1 cup whole wheat flour

½ cup all-purpose flour

½ teaspoon baking soda

¾ teaspoon salt

2 tablespoons unsalted butter, cold, cut into cubes

½ cup buttermilk

Place a rack in the center of the oven and preheat to 325 degrees F. Line 2 baking sheets with parchment paper. Set aside.

In a medium bowl, whisk together flaxseed, flaxseed meal, flours, baking soda, and salt. Add the butter, and using your fingers, quickly work the butter into the dry ingredients. Some of the butter will resemble oatmeal flakes; others will be the size of small pebbles. Make a well in the center of the mixture. Add the buttermilk, and use a fork to bring all of the ingredients together. Make sure that every bit of flour is moistened by the buttermilk. The dough will be shaggy.

Turn the dough out onto a lightly floured work surface and knead together about 10 times to bring the dough together. Wrap in plastic wrap and refrigerate for 10 minutes.

When chilled, cut dough in half. On a lightly floured work surface, with a lightly floured rolling pin, roll out half of the dough. Roll just thinner than ⅛ inch thick. Use a 1½-inch round cookie cutter to cut out crackers, or use a pizza cutter to trim the edges and cut the dough into 1½-inch squares. Prick each cracker with the tines of a fork and place on baking sheet.

Bake crackers for 15 to 18 minutes, until slightly browned around the edges. Remove from the oven and allow to cool completely before placing in an airtight container to store.

Crackers will last, in an airtight container, at room temperature for up to 4 days.

chewy coconut almond raisin granola bars

makes one 8-inch pan

If I make and eat these granola bars for an entire week straight, will I be able to fit into the sleek, backless dress I've had my eye on for weeks? Probably not. I don't think these are necessarily a diet solution, but they are super wholesome and filling.

These granola bars are on the chewy side, with crisp edges.

It's a wonderful recipe to share as a hostess gift or bake sale treat, especially considering that you can substitute any dried fruit or nut you'd like. Bake, wrap, and ribbon. It's that easy.

1½ cups old-fashioned or
quick-cooking oats
½ cup oat flour (see note)
½ cup packed brown sugar
2 tablespoons ground flaxseed meal

½ teaspoon salt
½ teaspoon ground cinnamon
⅛ teaspoon ground ginger
1 cup shredded coconut
(sweetened or unsweetened)

1 cup golden raisins
½ cup slivered almonds
¼ cup plus 2 tablespoons honey
¼ cup (½ stick) butter, melted
1 tablespoon fresh orange juice

NOTE: make oat flour by putting oats in a spice grinder, food processor, or blender.

Place a rack in the center of the oven and preheat to 350 degrees F. Line an 8-inch-square baking dish with foil so that some foil hangs over the edges of the pan. Butter the foil. Set aside.

In a large bowl, combine oats, oat flour, sugar, flaxseed meal, salt, cinnamon, ginger, coconut, raisins, and almonds.

In a small bowl, whisk together honey, melted butter, and orange juice. Pour over the flour mixture and toss together with a fork. The mixture will be dry but still sticky. Blend together until all of the dry ingredients are moistened by the honey mixture.

Dump oat mixture into prepared baking dish. With clean, slightly oiled fingers, press the oat mixture into the dish until tight and solid in the pan. Bake for 35 to 40 minutes, or until browned around the edges. The baked granola will still be soft even after it's fully baked, but will harden as it cools.

Remove baked granola from the oven and cool for 30 minutes. Place the baking dish in the refrigerator for about an hour before slicing. This will help to further cool the bars and keep them from crumbling when sliced.

Use the overhanging foil flaps to remove the baked granola. Use a large, sharp knife to cut block into 12 bars. Wrap individually in plastic wrap and store in an airtight jar.

Granola bars will last, well wrapped, at room temperature for up to 2 weeks.

chocolate peanut butter whoopie pies

makes about 18 whoopie pies

Maybe I should have titled this book *All the Awesome Ways You Should Combine Peanut Butter and Chocolate* because I sure can think of a lot of ways.

These Whoopie Pies are just another vehicle by which to enjoy this heavenly combination. The cookies are slightly cakey, soft, and rich. The filling is fluffy and crunchy, and filled with salty peanut butter flavor. Oh, man!

I love to wrap these cookies individually and store them in the refrigerator. They're most delicious served cold.

For the cookies:
2 cups all-purpose flour
½ cup unsweetened cocoa powder
1¼ teaspoons baking soda
1 teaspoon salt
1 teaspoon instant espresso powder
    (optional)
½ cup (1 stick) unsalted butter,
    softened

½ cup granulated sugar
½ cup packed brown sugar
1 large egg
2 teaspoons pure vanilla extract
1 cup buttermilk
For the filling:
½ cup (1 stick) unsalted butter,
    softened

1 (7-ounce) container
    marshmallow creme
½ cup smooth all-natural
    peanut butter
Pinch of salt
1 cup powdered sugar
1 teaspoon pure vanilla extract
¼ cup coarsely chopped roasted
    and salted peanuts

Place a rack in the upper third of the oven and preheat to 350 degrees F. Line a baking sheet with parchment paper. Set aside.

To make the cookies: in a medium bowl, whisk together flour, cocoa powder, baking soda, salt, and espresso powder. Set aside.

In the bowl of a stand mixer fitted with a paddle attachment, beat together butter and sugars until light and well incorporated, 3 to 5 minutes. Stop mixer and scrape down the sides of the bowl. Add the egg and beat on low speed for 1 minute, until mixture is light and fluffy. Beat in vanilla.

Stop the mixer and scrape down the sides of the bowl. Add half of the flour mixture and mix on low speed. With mixer running, slowly add the buttermilk. When just incorporated, add the remaining flour mixture. Mix until just blended. Finish incorporating the ingredients with a spatula.

Spoon the batter by the heaping tablespoonful onto prepared baking sheet. Leave at least an inch of space between the dough. Bake for 12 to 14 minutes, until centers are cooked through but cookies are still soft and tender.

Remove from oven and let cool on the pan for 10 minutes before removing to a wire rack to cool completely before filling.

To make the filling: in the bowl of an electric stand mixer fitted with a paddle attachment, beat together butter, marsh-mallow, peanut butter, and salt. Beat until smooth and no butter lumps remain. Add the powdered sugar and vanilla. Beat on medium speed for 3 minutes, until fluffy. Stop the mixer and remove the bowl. Fold in peanuts with a spatula.

When cookies have cooled, spread a scant 2 tablespoons of filling onto the bottom of one cookie. Top with another, similar-sized cookie. Fill all cookies and sandwich. Cookies are best wrapped individually in plastic wrap and stored in the refrigerator.

Whoopie Pies will last, well wrapped, in the refrigerator for up to 5 days.

browned butter peanut butter crispy rice treats

makes one 8-inch pan

Butter is good; browned butter is better. The only things in the world that could take traditional Rice Krispie Treats from good to better is browned butter and a healthy portion of peanut butter. These dessert blocks are absolutely delicious—but you probably already knew that. Browned butter deepens the flavor and peanut butter helps to cut down on the sweetness of the marshmallow. Make these and take all the credit. Please.

½ cup (1 stick) unsalted butter
1 (10-ounce) bag marshmallows, mini or large

½ cup smooth all-natural peanut butter
¼ teaspoon salt

6 cups (about half a box) crispy rice cereal

Butter an 8-inch-square baking pan. Set aside.

In a large, heavy-bottomed saucepan, melt butter over medium heat until just browned. Butter will melt, foam, and froth, then begin to brown along the bottom. Whisk browned bits off of the bottom of the pan.

Just as the butter begins to brown, add the marshmallows, peanut butter, and salt. Stir with a wooden spoon or spatula until mixture is silky smooth and speckled with browned butter bits. Remove pan from heat and add rice cereal. Quickly stir, ensuring that all of the cereal is coated in the marshmallow mixture.

Turn the mixture out into the prepared pan. With buttered or oiled fingertips, press mixture into the sides and bottom of the pan. Let cool and set for at least 30 minutes before slicing into 9 large blocks. Wrap individually in plastic wrap.

Crispy rice treats will last, well wrapped, at room temperature for up to 4 days.

honey mustard roasted cashews

makes 2 cups

Put honey mustard on anything and I'll want to eat it. It's a perfect sweet and spicy sauce. In this recipe, honey mustard is used to glaze already indulgent, buttery and fatty nuts. These cashews are such a perfect party snack or hostess gift, despite the fact that they're just a touch sticky. Go ahead and lick your fingers—it's totally okay.

¼ cup honey

1 tablespoon vegetable oil

1 to 2 teaspoons ground, dried mustard

2 cups roasted and salted cashews

½ teaspoon coarsely ground black pepper

Place a rack in the center of the oven and preheat oven to 375 degrees F. Line a baking sheet with parchment paper. Set aside.

In a medium bowl, whisk together honey, oil, and mustard. Add cashews to the bowl, and toss to coat. Fold until every nut is coated in the honey mixture.

Spread nuts out into a single layer on the prepared baking sheet. Top with black pepper and bake for 15 to 20 minutes, removing the nuts once or twice during baking to toss. Remove from oven and cool. Once cool, store in an airtight container.

Nuts will last, in an airtight container, at room temperature for up to 1 week.

meyer lemon curd

makes about 1 cup

Meyer Lemon Curd is delicate and fragrant, sweet and sour. In a little jar decorated with a ribbon, this makes such an elegant gift. With beautiful seasonal citrus and fresh eggs, curd always feels impressive. No one has to know that this curd is so simple to make.

½ cup fresh Meyer lemon juice (from
    2 to 3 lemons)
⅓ cup granulated sugar

2 large eggs
2 large egg yolks
Big pinch of salt

½ cup (1 stick) unsalted butter

Place a fine-mesh strainer over a medium bowl. Set aside for later.

In a medium, heavy-bottomed saucepan, whisk together lemon juice, sugar, eggs, yolks, and salt over medium-low heat. Whisk and heat until egg yolks have thickened the mixture. The mixture will go from smelling like citrus to smelling distinctly like lemon curd.

When thickened and fragrant, immediately remove from the heat, and whisk in the butter. Use a spatula to pour the warm curd into the strainer fit over the bowl. Use a spatula to move the curd through the strainer, leaving any cooked egg bits in the strainer. Pour strained curd into a small, airtight jar and refrigerate until chilled. Serve over biscuits or toast.

Meyer Lemon Curd will last, in an airtight container, in the refrigerator for up to 4 days.

vanilla bean snickerdoodles

makes about 2 dozen cookies

Some cookies are just simple wonders. These cookies are stacked with the flavors of vanilla and cinnamon. Sometimes cookies should be simple, but create a very tall stack. Don't you agree?

For the cookies:
2¾ cups all-purpose flour
2 teaspoons cream of tartar
1 teaspoon baking soda
¼ teaspoon salt

1 cup (2 sticks) unsalted butter, softened
1½ cups granulated sugar
2 large eggs
1 teaspoon pure vanilla extract

½ vanilla bean, scraped of seeds
For the topping:
1 teaspoon ground cinnamon
⅓ cup granulated sugar

To make the cookies: in a medium bowl, whisk together flour, cream of tartar, baking soda, and salt. Set aside.

In the bowl of an electric stand mixer fitted with a paddle attachment, beat together the butter and sugar until light and fluffy, 3 to 5 minutes. Stop mixer and scrape down the bowl. Beat in eggs on medium speed, one at a time, beating for 1 minute between additions. Beat in vanilla extract and bean.

Stop mixer and scrape down the bowl. Add flour mixture and beat on low speed until just incorporated. Stop the mixer, remove the bowl, and finish incorporating ingredients with a spatula. Refrigerate dough, in the bowl, for 30 minutes.

Place a rack in the upper third of the oven and preheat to 350 degrees F. Line a baking sheet with parchment paper. Set aside.

To make the topping: in a small bowl, toss together cinnamon and sugar. Spoon dough into heaping tablespoonfuls and roll in the cinnamon sugar mixture. Place on prepared baking sheet and bake for 12 to 14 minutes, until slightly browned around the edges. Remove from oven and cool cookies on baking sheet for 10 minutes before removing to a wire rack to cool completely.

Snickerdoodles will last, in an airtight container, at room temperature for up to 3 days.

lavender lemon bars

makes one 9x13-inch pan

Sneaking little bits of uncooked, buttery crust is a totally reasonable action to take when making these lemon bars. They're buttery, sweet, and full of bright citrus flavor. The lavender has a really lovely, floral accent. Also, I think lavender and yellow look pretty together. Sometimes it's as simple as that.

For the crust:

1 cup (2 sticks) unsalted butter, softened

¾ cup granulated sugar

¼ cup packed brown sugar

2 cups all-purpose flour

Pinch of salt

½ teaspoon dried lavender

For the lemon filling:

4 large eggs

1½ cups sugar

6 tablespoons all-purpose flour

½ cup fresh lemon juice (from 2 to 3 lemons)

2 teaspoons lemon zest

Powdered sugar and dried lavender for topping

Place a rack in the center of the oven and preheat to 350 degrees F. Butter a 9x13-inch pan and set aside.

To make the crust: in the bowl of a stand mixer fitted with a paddle attachment, beat together butter and sugars until pale and fluffy, 3 to 5 minutes. Stop the mixer, scrape down the bowl and add flour, salt, and lavender. Beat on low speed until dough just comes together. Stop the mixer, remove the bowl, and incorporate the rest of the ingredients with a spatula.

Dump the crust mixture into the prepared pan, and use your fingertips to press the dough into the bottom of the pan. Bake for 18 to 20 minutes, until slightly browned.

To make the filling: while the crust is baking, in a medium bowl, whisk together eggs and sugar until light and pale. Add flour, lemon juice, and lemon zest. Whisk until completely blended and incorporated.

Remove the baked crust from the oven and immediately pour the prepared filling over the hot crust. Return to the oven and bake for 20 to 25 minutes, until browned around the edges and no longer jiggly in the center.

Cool completely in the pan. Cut into wedges and dust with sifted powdered sugar and dried lavender buds. To store lemon bars, place in an airtight container in layers, separated by waxed paper.

Lavender Lemon Bars will last, in an airtight container, in the refrigerator for up to 4 days.

honey whole wheat pound cake

makes one 9x5-inch loaf

Honey and whole wheat are a winning combination. This loaf feels like part breakfast, part healthy snack, part dessert.

2¼ cups white whole wheat flour

2 teaspoons baking powder

½ teaspoon baking soda

1 teaspoon salt

¾ cup (1½ sticks) unsalted butter, softened

1 cup granulated sugar

½ cup honey

3 large eggs

2 teaspoons vanilla extract

1 cup buttermilk

Place a rack in the center of the oven and preheat to 350 degrees F. Butter and flour a 9x5-inch loaf pan. Set aside.

In a large bowl, whisk together flour, baking powder, baking soda, and salt. Set aside.

In the bowl of an electric stand mixer fitted with a paddle attachment, beat together butter, sugar, and honey until soft and creamy, 3 to 5 minutes. Stop the mixer and scrape down the bowl. On low speed, beat in the eggs, one at a time, beating for 1 minute between each addition. Beat in the vanilla.

With the mixer on low speed, beat in half of the flour mixture. Slowly add the buttermilk and beat until just incorporated. Add the remaining dry ingredients and beat until almost no flour bits remain. Stop the mixer and remove the bowl. Finish incorporating the batter with a spatula.

Spoon batter into prepared pan and bake for 55 to 65 minutes, or until a skewer inserted into the center of the cake comes out clean. Remove from oven and allow to cool in the pan for 20 minutes, before inverting onto a wire rack to cool completely.

Pound cake will last, wrapped in plastic wrap or foil, at room temperature for up to 4 days. Cake will also last, well wrapped, in the freezer for up to a month.

apple pie crostadas

makes 8 crostadas

Apple Pie Crostadas are a fist-sized version of apple pie. Topped with vanilla ice cream, they're just dreamy.

For the topping:

¼ cup all-purpose flour

¼ cup granulated sugar

Pinch of salt

¼ cup ground cinnamon

⅛ cup freshly ground nutmeg

⅛ teaspoon ground allspice

¼ cup (½ stick) unsalted butter, cold, cut into cubes

For the crust:

1½ cups all-purpose flour

2 tablespoons granulated sugar

¾ teaspoon salt

½ cup (1 stick) unsalted butter, cold, cut into cubes

¼ cup cold water

For the filling:

4 Granny Smith apples

¼ cup packed brown sugar

1 tablespoon all-purpose flour

½ teaspoon ground cinnamon

2 teaspoons fresh lemon juice

½ teaspoon lemon zest

For the egg wash:

1 egg

¼ cup granulated sugar

To make the topping: in a medium bowl, whisk together flour, sugar, salt, and spices. Add butter and, working quickly, use your fingers to incorporate the butter into the dry ingredients. Some of the butter will be the size of oats, others will be the size of small pebbles. Place in a small bowl and place in the refrigerator until ready to use.

To make the crust: in the same medium bowl used to prepare the topping, combine the flour, sugar, and salt. Add the butter and use your fingers to quickly incorporate the butter. Some butter bits will be the size of oats; others the size of small pebbles.

Create a well in the center of the bowl and add the water. Use a fork to bring the wet and dry ingredients together. Make sure all of the flour mixture is moistened and turn out onto a lightly floured work surface. Knead 5 to 10 times just to bring the ingredients together into a disk. Wrap in plastic wrap and refrigerate for an hour.

To make the filling: while the dough chills, peel and core the apples. Slice into even, thin wedges and place in a medium bowl. Add sugar, flour, cinnamon, lemon juice, and zest, and toss with a wooden spoon. Let stand, at room temperature, until the crust is ready to be rolled out. The apples will macerate and create juice. That's just what we want!

Place a rack in the center of the oven and preheat to 400 degrees F. Line 2 baking sheets with parchment paper and set aside.

Remove the chilled dough from the fridge and use a knife to cut the dough into 8 even portions. Place 1 piece of dough onto a lightly floured work surface. With a lightly floured rolling pin, roll dough to a round, ¼-inch thickness. Set aside until all dough pieces are rolled out. Place 4 dough rounds on each baking sheet.

For the egg wash: with a fork, beat egg. Using a pastry brush, lightly brush the top of each dough with egg wash. Fill with about ⅓ cup of apple filling and juices. Sprinkle about 2 tablespoons of topping on top of the apples and fold dough up around the apples, pinching and crimping. Brush each crust lightly with egg wash and sprinkle with sugar.

Bake crostadas for 10 to 20 minutes, until golden brown and bubbly. Remove from the oven. Allow to cool on the pan for 15 minutes, before serving. Crostadas are lovely served warm with vanilla ice cream.

Crostadas are best served the day they're made, though they will last, in an airtight container, in the refrigerator for up to 3 days. Reheat, wrapped in foil in a 300 degree F oven for 15 minutes.

if you have the power
to coax something
beautifully sweet
out of your kitchen,
it's as though you
have a magic wand
in your hands

acknowledgments

Well, heck! I wrote a cookbook! My name is on the cover, but I surely didn't do this alone.

Thank you, big hugs, high fives, and cheers to:

Mom and Dad—Thank you for letting me steal all of your cake pans, bake in your fancy oven, and do all of my laundry at your house. One day I'll be a grown-up, I'm just not sure when.

Michael—Thank you for diving into this project with me. Thank you for letting me freak out at you on occasion. Thank you for fixing my hair and fixing my photos. Your friendship is the reason that this book exists.

The Sanitarium—Much of the baking and photography in this book took place at the Sanitarium, a beautiful home and bed and breakfast in San Luis Obispo, California. Thank you Susie, Vincent, and Suzanne for your generosity, kindness, and support.

Lauren and Launa—Sisters are friends forever. Thank you for that.

Rachel and Whitney—We eat, drink, and dream big together. You inspire me!

Mommom and Papa, Dan and Judy, Larry and Debbie—Thank you for loving me even when I was big-toothed, frizzy haired, bratty, and annoying. Your love and support created this. I love you!

Thank you Alison and Leslie. Awesome agent. Awesome editor. You make me look good.

Thank you Tracy Shutterbean and Hilton Carter. I love you from deep down on the inside of things.

Thank YOU—for reading this book, for baking from this book, and for reading my blog so loyally. You have fundamentally changed my life. I am so thankful for the community that we have created. You inspire me every day. Thank you!

index

in the kitchen,
it's emotion that inspires somethi[ng]
beautiful and delicious